# Personal Money Management

*Methods for Self-Improvement*

## THOMAS HURLEY

Co-authored with

### RAYMOND AARON

AuthoritiesPress

Personal Money Management: Methods of Self-Improvement

www.PersonalMoneyManagement.club

Publisher
10-10-10 Publishing
Markham, ON
Canada

Printed in Canada and the United States of America

# Table of Contents

# Acknowledgments

Life is never a one-person event. We are dependent on one another to inspire and encourage each of us to do better than we think we can. The use of mentors, teachers and advice from others is essential as you cannot go it alone. I would like to thank all the people in my life, including teachers, managers of companies, co-workers as well as authors of the many books I have read. Some of my mentors are:

My parents **Richard** and **Norah Hurley**, who led me down the right path and instilled good work ethics. They had the foresight and courage to emigrate to the great country of Canada. Working on a small family farm was awesome even though it was hard work. We certainly learned where our food came from and how it is made. The 4H farm club taught many skills that I have used in my life.

**Raymond Aaron** and The Raymond Aaron Group, who have provided not only the inspiration but also the mechanics behind completing this book. What an awesome group of people they are and they opened up my eyes to the opportunities around the world and the people that are changing it.

**Clayton Bye**, who helped write, edit and format this book. His experience was very beneficial to the finished product.

The people and the country of Canada for instilling so much pride in me and our nation. We are some of the best peacekeepers in the world. We are respected worldwide and do not have to carry guns in fear of our safety. During the pandemic that came in the first quarter of the year 2020, we had good hospitals and medical services to look after our people. All of our other services in transportation, police, fire and food were kept up in an orderly fashion.

# Foreword

Thomas Hurley is the kind of guy you want to have in your corner. He understands finances because he has been in the trenches. He has also studied what he's talking about in this book, *Personal Money Management*. From budgeting and your own net worth statement to the intricacies of the financial marketplace, Thomas identifies the basics you need to manage your money. Why is this so important? No one, and I mean no one, will look after your money better than you will—if you are armed with solid basics and an understanding of how the financial world works.

Thomas learned a lot about the financial world working with multi-millionaire Raymond Aaron in the real estate market. He has also studied that world close up and in detail. He's still doing so.

But there's no substituting actual experience. Thomas knows that what he has written about works. It has been proven by him and a litany of others. You can take that to the bank. I make millionaires; Thomas gives you the opportunity to begin such a journey yourself, with a solid base and a plan of action.

Managing your assets and your liabilities is definitely a great place to begin wealth accumulation. Yet Thomas will take you further; he'll walk you through many different ways to leverage yourself financially. This is the sign of a true teacher. He'll set your feet firmly on the ground, and then he will stretch you. He'll take you out of your comfort zone.

I can't say how much I think Thomas has given you a blueprint of the financial world, and how much he has offered the layperson that has often remained just out of his or her grasp. He won't steer you wrong.

Loral Langemeier
*The Millionaire Maker*

# Must Read First!

This book is about the average, everyday person who was not born rich and may not even know the value of their net worth. Net worth is your assets minus your liabilities. A lot of the people in the middle class may never have figured out their net worth. It's up to the individual to look after their financial management. This book is mainly for the Canadian market but a lot of it also applies in the USA.

One of the things I know is that some form of accounting is necessary and you have to do the accounting or else someone, maybe the government, will do it for you. Most of you will have to pay taxes and the government will NOT do the best job of looking after your tax credits. I recommend that you get your income and expenses together and engage an accountant or as a minimum a bookkeeper that files income tax for you. The reason is income tax changes from year to year and the layman doesn't keep up with the changes.

One money-saving idea is to operate a small business out of your home. You need income but your expenses can exceed your income for several years and can be carried backward as well as forward. With any of these ideas you have to keep accurate records as you may be audited by the government, and you must have the documentation and preferably help to fight the government and recover all the tax that should be returned to you.

Another tax credit a lot of people miss is a disability tax credit which is available for many illnesses as well as disabilities. You have to check with a knowledgeable individual but anything that affects daily living (ADL) may have a tax credit. I have a tax credit for an ankle fused because of arthritis. The tax credit was for $6000 which gave me a return of $2000 in the year I filed. One big advantage was this credit goes on for the rest of my life and I don't have to reapply every year. Some examples of disabilities are arthritis, diabetes and mental problems as well as obvious physical impairment. Some people also qualify for disability grants which is tax-free money from the government. All of these ideas have to be applied for with the government and may be different from province to province or state to state.

Some of the things you may have to look after are your bank account, credit, investments, housing management, clothing and groceries. In today's society most people don't write the cheques that we used to write. With the use of debit cards, it's more important now that one looks after their bank account balance. And this naturally leads to a discussion regarding the number one thing that affects your bank account: credit.

# Chapter 1

# Credit

It's essential to look after your credit, which is defined as the ability to borrow money or access goods or services with the understanding that you'll pay later. So, it's startling that few people know their credit score. Equifax and Trans Union are two of the companies that banks use to get your credit score. Your credit report generates a number between 300 and 900 with the higher number being better. This report also gives your payment history, length of credit and several other things that banks use. It shows the amount you can borrow as well as the amount you have borrowed and from who you have borrowed it.

PAC (Pre-authorized Contribution) is a plan where payments are automatically deducted money from your bank account. It is set up by the merchant to make automatic monthly payments for things like utilities, life insurance and other purchases that come every month. A problem arises when your balance is too low and the payment is not taken out because the account is NSF (not sufficient funds). This creates extra expense and time for the bank and the merchant and you'll be assessed extra fees by both. The amount over can just be pennies, but the charge will go NSF and be sent back to the merchant. To prevent this from happening you can set an overdraft loan but it's advisable to use this as little as possible. If you have payments go NSF it will affect your credit rating.

Something else you have to look after is any money you may have in different investment vehicles. If you invest in real estate you have to manage the building somehow. If it's stocks and bonds or other securities, you still need to keep an eye on where the investment is going even though you have investment advisors.

Regarding loans, banks are usually looking for an income ratio of between 36 to 43% and also a mortgage ratio of less than 28%. Banks also look at the amount of life insurance you have. Some mortgages require mortgage insurance.

It's a good idea to use credit cards and pay the bills regularly so as to establish a credit rating. If you never use your credit you may not qualify for a larger loan as you won't have a credit rating. This idea is important because, for a young person to establish good habits, you must have proof that you're responsible and pay your bills consistently.

## Debt-to-Income Ratio

The debt-to-income (DTI) ratio is a personal finance measure that compares an individual's monthly debt payment to his or her monthly gross income. Your gross income is your pay before taxes and other deductions are taken out. The debt-to-income ratio is the percentage of your gross monthly income that goes to paying your monthly debt payments.

## DTI Formula and Calculation

The DTI ratio is one of the metrics that lenders, including mortgage lenders, use to measure an individual's ability to manage monthly payments and repay debts.

1. Sum up your monthly debt payments including credit cards, loans, and mortgage.

2. Divide your total monthly debt payment amount by your monthly gross income.

3. The result will yield a decimal, so multiply the result by 100 to achieve your DTI percentage.

**(Debt Payment $_____ / Monthly Gross Income
$_____) x 100 = Debt to Income ratio _____%**

## What Does the DTI Ratio Tell You?

A low debt-to-income (DTI) ratio demonstrates a good balance between debt and income. In other words, if your DTI ratio is 15%, that means that 15% of your monthly gross income goes to debt payments each month. Conversely, a high DTI ratio can signal that an individual has too much debt for the amount of income earned each month.

Typically, borrowers with low debt-to-income ratios are likely to manage their monthly debt payments effectively. As a result, banks and financial credit providers want to see low DTI ratios before issuing loans to a potential borrower. The preference for low DTI ratios makes sense since lenders want to be sure a borrower isn't overextended, meaning they have too many debt payments relative to their income.

As a general guideline, 43% is the highest DTI ratio a borrower can have and still qualify for a mortgage. Ideally, lenders prefer a debt-to-income ratio lower than 36%, with no more than 28% of that debt going towards servicing a mortgage or rent payment.

The maximum DTI ratio varies from lender to lender. However, the lower the debt-to-income ratio, the better the chances that the borrower will be approved, or at least considered, for the credit application.

## Debt-to-Income Ratio Limitations

Although important, the DTI ratio is only one financial ratio or metric used in making a credit decision. A borrower's credit history and credit score will also weigh heavily in a decision to extend credit to a borrower. A credit score is a numeric value of your ability to pay back a debt. Several factors impact a score negatively or positively, and they include late payments, delinquencies, number of open credit accounts, balances on credit cards relative to their credit limits or credit utilization.

The DTI ratio does not distinguish between different types of debt and the cost of servicing that debt. Credit cards carry higher interest rates than student loans, but they're lumped in together in the DTI ratio calculation. If you transferred your balances from your high-interest rate cards to a low-interest credit card, your monthly payments would decrease. As a result, your total monthly debt payments and your DTI ratio would decrease, but your total debt outstanding would remain unchanged.

The debt-to-income ratio is an important ratio to monitor when applying for credit, but it's only one metric used by lenders in making a credit decision.

The DTI ratio can also be used to measure the percentage of income that goes toward housing costs, which for renters is the monthly rent amount. Lenders look to see if a potential borrower can manage their current debt load while paying their rent on time, given their gross income.

## Mortgage Ratios

These help you determine whether or not you can qualify for a home mortgage based on income and expenses. To qualify for a mortgage loan at a bank, you will need to pass a "stress test." You will need to prove you can afford payments at a qualifying interest rate which is typically higher than the actual rate in your mortgage contract. Credit unions and other lenders that aren't federally regulated don't need to use this mortgage stress test. The qualifying interest rate your lender will use for the stress test depends on whether you need to get mortgage loan insurance. If you need mortgage loan insurance, the bank must use the higher interest rate of either the Bank of Canada's conventional five-year mortgage rate or the interest rate you negotiate with your lender. If you don't need mortgage loan insurance, the bank must use the higher interest rate of either the Bank of Canada's conventional five-year mortgage rate or the interest rate you negotiate with your lender plus 2%.

## Property Information

| | |
|---|---|
| Property Value | $_____ |
| Down Payment | $_____ |
| Annual Interest Rate | _____ percent |
| Amortization Period | _____ years |
| Payment Frequency | _____ |
| Term | _____ years |
| Your Gross Income | $_____ per month |
| Heating Cost | $_____ per month |
| Property Taxes | $_____ per month |
| Credit Card/Line of Credit | $_____ per month |
| Car Payment | $_____ per month |
| Other Debt Payment | $_____ per month |

**(Monthly Expenses $_____ / Monthly Income $_____) x 100 = Gross Debt Service ratio (GDS) _____ percent**

**(Annual Mortgage Payment $_____ + Property Taxes $_____ + Other Debt Payments $_____ / Gross Family Income $_____) x 100 = Total Debt Service ratio (TDS) _____ percent**

FCAC (Financial Consumer Agency of Canada) uses a Gross Debt Service (GDS) ratio of 32% and a Total Debt Service (TDS) ratio of 40% in this tool as a guideline. You may still qualify for a mortgage even if your GDS and TDS ratios are slightly higher. However, higher GDS and TDS ratios mean that you are increasing the risk of taking on more debt than you can afford.

## What's Your Net Worth?

Find out your net worth—the difference between **what you own** (your assets) and **what you owe** (your liabilities). Understanding that difference is a great way to help you plan for the future.

*Your household assets:*

### (A) Your savings and investments:

| | |
|---|---|
| Registered retirement savings: | $_____ |
| Tax-free savings accounts (TFSA): | $_____ |
| Non-registered savings and investments: | $_____ |
| **Total (A)** | $_____ |

### (B) Your property and other assets:

| | |
|---|---|
| Home value: | $_____ |
| Other properties: | $_____ |
| Vehicle(s): | $_____ |
| Other valuables: | $_____ |
| **Total (B)** | $_____ |

*Your household liabilities:*

**(C) Liabilities**

Home mortgage:                                    $_____

Other mortgages:                                  $_____

Credit cards:                                     $_____

Lines of credit:                                  $_____

Loans:                                            $_____

**Total (C)**                                     $_____

**(Total A + Total B) – Total C = Net Worth**
($_____ + $_____ ) - $_____ = $_____

**Nouveau Riche** is someone who has recently become wealthy and enjoys spending money. The term nouveau riche is a derogatory term meant to mock people who have a great deal of money but don't have the good taste to spend it in a "classy" way. The inference is that it's more socially acceptable to inherit money and the ageless traditions that often go with it than to suddenly become wealthy.

The comparison between "old money" and "new money" is one that is often made. Old money is usually wealth that's inherited from your family. New money is wealth that's come from one's own business, the lottery, stocks, trades or being a celebrity. In other words, you have first-generation wealth.

Who are some of the nouveau riche who come to mind? My favourite is F. Scott Fitzgerald's fictional The Great Gatsby. Think of flashy lifestyle, grandiose parties, expensive cars and a high profile.

In contrast, people with old money tend to live with understated elegance, and class and retention of funds are their catchwords.

I tend to think of the dressed-down neighbour who has a modest home and an ugly truck but who is worth millions. But the prevailing view of old money is of people who are elitist or have a superior attitude.

These are two very opposing schools of thought when it comes to financial habits and view of wealth. Just because you have "made it" and have enough wealth to last you a lifetime, you aren't guaranteed financial success. It really depends on having a balanced view of short- and long-term financial goals.

The main concern for the nouveau riche is that they have a short-term view of their wealth. It's not uncommon for these people to spend all their wealth in a matter of years, resulting in bankruptcy or a life of endless debt.

The point, of course, is that your relationship with money can be self-determined. It's mostly dependent on your view of success and your ability to practice financial habits that ensure your long-term security. Why not take a balanced approach, learning to enjoy your wealth but also ensuring your long-term financial success?

## The Difference Between Banks and Credit Unions

The following descriptions can help you decide whether to use a bank or a credit union for your financial needs.

### Profit Versus Non-Profit

Banks are for-profit organizations, and every transaction made is meant to make a profit (in addition to providing a service to customers). Earnings are paid back to both members and stockholders. Banks make money by lending funds at interest rates that are higher than the cost of the money deposited in the bank. They also make money from securities they own.

Credit unions are not-for-profit institutions, and they operate to serve their members. They pay dividends to their members.

## Regulations

The federal government oversees banks. The Bank Act legislates them.

Most credit unions are governed by the province in which they reside. They are also legislated by the Bank Act.

## Customers

There's no real difference between the types of customers that are served by banks versus credit unions. However, credit unions tend to be more rural and have stricter rules.

Membership also tends to require the purchase of a share and the ability to meet other requirements. Shareholder members are given the power to voter regarding how the institution is operated. Shareholders at banks are typically investors.

## Account Types

Credit unions and banks "sell" the same types of products, but banks can offer more variety. In addition, banks provide commercial loan products rather than the smaller consumer loans tendered by credit unions.

## Board Members

Credit unions boards are made up of volunteers who have been voted in by members. Bank board members are selected and paid by shareholders.

## ATM Machines and Other Services

Every banking institution has its own ATM (Automatic Teller Machine) and services. Credit unions often share their resources. Members are allowed to use the ATMs and services of other credit unions. This is true, no matter the location. They also offer those services free of charge, provided they're part of the same financial institution. Sometimes fees are charged by ATMs from other institutions.

## Fees

The fees that banks charge their clients are usually higher than those charged by credit unions. Credit unions also may issue dividends from profits to members, but banks only issue dividends to stockholders.

For further help with credit issues, contact Thomas Hurley at **tombhur@gmail.com**.

**Notes**

_____

_____

_____

_____

_____

_____

_____

_____

_____

_____

_____

_____

_____

_____

_____

_____

_____

_____

_____

_____

## Notes

# Chapter 2

# Budget

**B**udgeting is defined as the process of creating a plan to spend your money. By creating a spending plan you gain the ability to determine in advance whether you'll have enough money to do the things you need and want to do.

A budget is formed by balancing your expenses with your income. If they don't balance, and you spend more than you make, you'll have a problem. Many people don't realize that they spend more than they earn and slowly sink deeper into debt every year.

## Why is budgeting important?

Budgeting ensures that you'll always have enough money for the things you need and those that are important to you. It will also keep you out of debt or help you work your way out of debt.

## Using a budget to forecast

Once you have a budget in place, you may want to map out your spending for six months to a year down the road. This allows you to forecast which months your finances may be tight and which ones you'll have extra money. You can then look for ways to even out the highs and lows in your finances so that things can be more manageable and pleasant.

Extending your budget out into the future also allows you to forecast how much money you will be able to save for important things like your vacation, a new vehicle, your first home or home renovations, an emergency savings account or your retirement. Using a realistic budget to forecast your spending for the year can really help you with your long-term financial planning. You can then make realistic assumptions about your annual income and expense and plan for long-term financial goals like starting your own business, buying an investment or recreation property or retiring.

Learn how to budget and create a spending plan.

## Groceries

Grocery bills can be reduced by several means. Careful planning is necessary, and carrying a list while shopping is crucial. Stores like No Frills and Costco offer substantial savings for large families. Some stores price match if you bring ads from other stores. Another money-saving idea is to buy meat at the end of the week, late on Fridays, so that there may be a reduction in the price because the store wants to get rid of the products before Sunday. Your grocery receipt should always be checked because cashiers often make mistakes. Some stores make their own bread at about a dollar a loaf compared to two or three dollars off the regular shelf. Store brand names usually are cheaper than the other brands. Going through flyers and comparing prices will save you some money.

## Couponing

One way of reducing grocery costs is through a good coupon program. To find that program go to YouTube and look up couponing. Couponing is done by looking in flyers for good deals on grocery items you redeem using the coupons at the grocery store. People have been known to get hundreds of dollars of groceries for sale for as little as five dollars. Advertisement matching is another money-saving idea. The use of loyalty programs is very important. Chains stores often have loyalty programs that are combined so that you get the maximum return. For example, Shoppers Drug Mart, The Real Canadian Superstore and No Frills are part of one chain and use the same loyalty program.

## Clothing

Clothing is another expensive item for families. Shopping discount stores like Walmart help save on these costs. People have found bargains at thrift stores, especially for children's clothing. This clothing may be used, but it's in good shape. I have even bought clothing at a thrift store, that was brand new but had the tags removed. Shopping sales like Black Friday are also a benefit. Back-to-school is another good time to buy clothing and school supplies, as is Christmas.

## Transportation

Transportation can be an expensive item. In the cities, a one-mile walk is not unreasonable. Automobiles and parking are some of the more expensive items, especially at hospitals and sporting events. Taking a taxi is very expensive, especially if it's for little children going to school every day. Rural areas have much greater problems with transportation as there are no subway or city bus systems. Ambulance is another transportation mode that's expensive and in short supply. Often people rely on relatives or neighbours for transportation to and from hospitals. Ambulance service can also be very poor in rural areas. The proliferation of toll highways is adding to transportation costs.

## Living Accommodations

Living accommodations are another important cost, depending on where you live. If you live in Toronto or any of the major cities, properties are very high priced and rent can be expensive. The cost of living accommodations can be a burdensome budget item. It depends upon the number of people in your family. You can often get shared facilities of some sort if you're single. Cheaper rent can often be found on Kijiji or Craigslist and in newspapers. Bus lines or subways may be necessary. And the nearer you get to bus lines, subways, beaches, waterfront, parks or sports fields the more expensive properties and rent become. Also the more facilities available—like gyms, swimming pools and elevators— the higher the rent or property value is. Condo living is more expensive than townhouses or semi-detached housing because you have condo fees for upkeep, as well as taxes and utilities. The major advantage of condos is that you don't have to do the maintenance.

## Entertainment

Entertainment is another thing that needs to be budgeted. One area of entertainment is reading, which also can increase your knowledge. Belonging to a library gives you access to many books, magazines, newspapers and free computer and internet usage. There are many courses that can be taken at a library, often free or for a small price. Hobbies and journaling are also entertainment. Service clubs and churches are some of the places that are entertainment as well as being educational. Some communities have garden plots available and you can learn to teach children about food. Gardening is also recreation and stress relief for some people.

## Emergencies

Planning for emergencies is a good idea. Having six month's rent or all expenses in an account will help you get by most emergencies. If you have family, you can often get help there as well. Emergencies bring extra stress, which can be debilitating. Sometimes there's government help that you can apply for. Hospitalization brings extra expenses, including additional transportation, parking at hospitals and personal care after discharge from hospital. This applies to patients as well as family that would like to come to visit. After discharge, some patients may require long-term care in a facility with rents in the $2,000 to $4,000 range. If the patient is the main wage earner, then the loss of income may be a big factor. Once the patient is at home there may be the cost of returning them to hospital or doctor's offices, as well as bandages and extra medication. Although there's a drug plan in the province of Ontario, I've had to pay an extra $500 a month for medication for my wife. This situation went on for several years and amounted to quite a cost.

## Retirement

Retirement is another thing that you should plan for. Starting early saving for retirement is very beneficial. Some of the places to look for help are life insurance agents, banks, stock brokers and financial planners. Primerica agents (www.primerica.com) and others have computer programs that will show how much you need to save to maintain the lifestyle you are used to. At one time $100,000 was a large amount, but now planning for 30 years down the road demonstrates that you need substantially more money than that.

Investments will be discussed in later chapters. The government feels that a person will only need about 65% of their current income to live on. What they don't say is if a person wants to retire early, then they have a longer retirement period. Some people only have government pensions and that doesn't give them a very good retirement. If you have some RRSPs, then these can be used to augment your retirement income. People often downsize their housing requirements, as hopefully they don't have dependent children still at home. Another strategy, if they want to stay in their house, is to do a reverse mortgage (to be talked about later). The greying of the population—more people getting older—causes many unforeseen problems. One of the problems that often comes up is the death of one of the spouse, which quite often means the income is greatly reduced. This phenomenon has caused many seniors to return to work in various lower paid jobs. Also, the lower income causes some people to have to find lower cost accommodation. Sometimes lower income people have higher health care costs.

Purchasing a house in your early working years is a big benefit as it may be paid off, leaving you with only tax and utility expenses. If you wanted to sell your house, chances are the value has probably gone up. At the moment the sale of the house that you live in wouldn't create a tax implication, and it would provide some cash to fund your retirement. This large amount of money could buy an annuity to take care of you for the rest of your life. Annuities will be covered in a later chapter.

What follows are examples of detailed monthly budgets for families and for businesses:

# Budget

**Name:** _____

**Income & Expenses for the month of** _____

## MONTHLY FAMILY INCOME (NET)

| | Husband | Spouse |
|---|---|---|
| Employment income | _____ | _____ |
| Pension/Annuities | _____ | _____ |
| Child support | _____ | _____ |
| Spousal support | _____ | _____ |
| Employment insurance benefits | _____ | _____ |
| Social assistance | _____ | _____ |
| Self-employment income | _____ | _____ |
| Child Tax Benefit | _____ | _____ |
| Other net income | _____ | _____ |
| **Total** | _____ | _____ |

## MONTHLY FAMILY NON-DISCRETIONARY EXPENSES

| | |
|---|---|
| Child support payments | _____ |
| Spousal support payments | _____ |
| Child care | _____ |
| Medical condition expenses | _____ |
| Fines/Penalties imposed by the court | _____ |
| Expenses as a condition of employment | _____ |
| Debts where stay has been lifted | _____ |
| Other expenses | _____ |
| **Total (A)** | _____ |

## MONTHLY FAMILY DISCRETIONARY EXPENSES

**Housing expenses**

| | |
|---|---|
| Rent/Mortgage | _____ |
| Property taxes/Condo fees | _____ |
| Heating/Gas/Oil | _____ |
| Telephone | _____ |
| Cable | _____ |
| Hydro | _____ |
| Water | _____ |
| Furniture | _____ |
| Other | _____ |

**Living expenses**

| | |
|---|---|
| Food/Grocery | _____ |
| Laundry/Dry cleaning | _____ |
| Grooming/Toiletries | _____ |
| Clothing | _____ |
| Other | _____ |

# Personal Money Management

**Personal expenses**

Smoking _____

Alcohol _____

Dining/Lunches/ _____
Restaurants

Entertainment/Sports _____

Gifts/Charitable _____
donations

Allowances _____

Other _____

**Non-recoverable
expenses**

Prescriptions _____

Dental _____

Other _____

**Transportation expenses**

Car lease/Payments _____

Repair/Maintenance/ _____
Gas

Public transportation _____

Other _____

**Insurance expenses**

Vehicle _____

House _____

Furniture/Contents _____

Life insurance _____

Other _____

**Payments**

To the estate _____

To secured Creditor _____
(other than mortgage
and vehicle)

Other _____

**Total (B)** _____

**Income Total:** _____

**Expense Total (A+B): (** _____ **)**

**Difference:** _____

26

# *Budget*

**Name:** _____

**Month:** _____


**BUSINESS INCOME**     [_____]

Gross Income     [_____]

**BUSINESS EXPENSE**     [_____]

Advertising     [_____]

Bad debts     [_____]

Tax, fees, licences, dues, memberships     [_____]

Fuel costs (except for motor vehicles)     [_____]

Insurance     [_____]

Interest     [_____]

Maintenance and repairs     [_____]

Management and administration fees     [_____]

Meals and entertainment     [_____ x 50% =] [_____]

Vehicle:

     Gas & Oil

     Maintenance     [_____]

     Insurance     [_____]

     Licence     [_____]

     Capital cost allowance     [_____]

     Interest     [_____]

     CAA     [_____]

     Other car expenses     [_____]

Purchases during year     [_____]

Office expenses     [_____]

Supplies     [_____]

Legal, accounting & other professional services     [_____]

Property taxes     [_____]

Rent     [_____]

Sales, wages & benefits     [_____]

Travel     [_____]

Telephone & utilities     [_____]

Convention fees     [_____]

Private health plan premiums     [_____]

*Personal Money Management*

| | |
|---|---|
| Reserves | |
| Terminal loss | |
| Other 1. _____ | |
| 2. _____ | |
| 3. _____ | |
| Capital cost allowance | |
| Capital cost allowance (leases & franchises) | |
| **Total Business Expenses** | |

**Business Use of Home Expenses**

| | |
|---|---|
| Percent used for business | % |
| Expenses: | |
| Heat | |
| Electricity | |
| Insurance | |
| Maintenance | |
| Mortgage Interest | |
| Property taxes | |
| Total | |
| Business Use of Home Percentage | ( %) |

| | |
|---|---|
| **Business Income – Gross** | $ |
| **Total Business Expenses** | ( ) |
| Subtotal | |
| Tax Deduction Rate | ( %) |
| Tax Deduction Amount | ( ) |
| **Net Monthly Income** | $ |

Questions regarding budgeting? Contact Thomas Hurley at **tombhur@gmail.com**.

## *Notes*

_____

_____

_____

_____

_____

_____

_____

_____

_____

_____

_____

_____

_____

_____

_____

_____

_____

_____

_____

_____

_____

_____

## Notes

_____

_____

_____

_____

_____

_____

_____

_____

_____

_____

_____

_____

_____

_____

_____

_____

_____

_____

# Chapter 3

# Insurance

## Insurance

There are various types of insurance, and you need to know some of the types and what they do. Contents of both your house or your apartment need to be insured in case of fire or theft so that you can replace them. The contents of an apartment could run into several thousand dollars, but the contents of a house can run into many, many thousands of dollars. Content insurance is relatively cheap.

With **houses** you have to insure the structure and cover any liability should someone get hurt on your property. There are two ways to determine how much insurance to carry on your house. One way is replacement value and the other is for a set amount. Replacement value may be more expensive because the price of your property may go up every year. Also you may have done improvements, which increases the value of the property. Liability covers you if someone were to get hurt on your property—either as a visitor or as somebody doing some work on the house.

**Car insurance** is necessary if you have a vehicle. Before you license your car or truck, you have to place insurance on it. Government determines the minimum amount, but you can buy more insurance than the minimum by paying extra premiums. If you were to get into a bad accident, you could be liable for many thousands of dollars in damages. Automobile insurance also has fire, theft, liability and collision. Fire and theft are self-explanatory, liability pays if you get in an accident and damage another person's car, and collision pays for damage to your car. None of these insurances are guaranteed to pay if you are impaired by alcohol or drugs.

**Life insurance** comes in three different ideologies. Some of the reasons you may want insurance on your person is to leave your spouse and children some money so they're not in a financial bind if you pass away. You may also want insurance to cover any debt that you've accumulated at this point in life.

I recommend term life insurance as it is the cheapest policy to cover your liabilities in case of death. The face amount, which is how much you want, is determined by what you want to pass on to your next of kin. This amount will vary at different times of your life, as your circumstances change. Whole life is also available, which supposedly is a savings plan as well as insurance, but it has not served people well over the long term. Universal life plans pair a combination of term and whole life and has also not served very well over the long term.

## Car Insurance

**Auto insurance** is a policy you purchase to help defer costs associated with getting into an auto accident. Instead of having to pay for auto accidents, you make annual premium payments to an insurance company. The company will then pay all or most of the costs associated with an accident or other vehicle damage.

**Premiums** will vary depending on your age, gender, years of driving experience, accident history, traffic violations and other factors. Provinces mandate that vehicle owners must buy a minimum amount of insurance. However, you can obtain additional coverage to protect yourself further.

Two things can raise your premiums: a poor driving record or the purchase of complete coverage. However, you can lower those payments by agreeing to take on more risk. This is done by raising your deductible.

**Coverages** are paid by your insurance company in exchange for the premium you pay. They include:

- **Property**—will pay for damage to your car. It also covers theft.

- **Liability**—will pay any legal responsibility you have to others for bodily injury or property damage, up to the maximum outlined in your policy.

- **Medical**—will pay the costs of treating your injuries, rehabilitation and sometimes lost wages and funeral expenses.

Within limits set by the government and the insurer, you can customize your policy to suit your needs and budget. Terms are usually one year and are renewable. Most policies may also be paid automatically on a monthly basis.

If you're buying your vehicle on credit, the lender may require more than the minimum of **Personal Liability and Property Damage (PLPD)** required by the province:

- **Bodily injury liability**—covers costs associated with injuries or death that you or another driver causes while driving your car.

- **Property damage liability**—reimburses others for damage that you or another driver operating your car causes to another vehicle or other property.

Provinces may also require:

- **Medical payments or personal injury protection**— which provides reimbursement for medical expenses for injuries to you or your passengers. It may also cover lost wages and other related expenses.

- **Uninsured motorist coverage**—Reimburses you when an accident is caused by a driver who doesn't have his or her own auto insurance.

> **Note:** Personal auto insurance won't provide coverage if you use your car for commercial purposes. Nor will it provide coverage if you use your car to work for ride-sharing services such as Uber or Lyft. Although, some auto insurers now offer supplemental insurance products that extend coverage for vehicle owners who provide ride-sharing services.

## Home Insurance

**Home insurance** protects your house and the contents against financial loss if they're damaged, lost or stolen (in exchange for annual premiums). Home insurance can also cover living expenses if you can't live in your home for a while due to an insured loss. Most policies insure you against financial liability in case someone is injured on your property, or if you cause damage to someone else's property—to the maximums outlined in your policy.

## Types of policies

- **No-frills** provides coverage to properties that don't meet normal insurance standards.

- **Standard** only covers events and occurrences that may put your home at risk that are specifically stated in the policy.

- **Broad** covers more than a standard policy but less than a comprehensive policy.

- **Comprehensive** covers your building, personal liability and all other risks.

The amount of coverage you need is determined by such factors as the worth of your home and its contents, the age of the house and where it's situated, and the risk you represent to the insurer. There are several types of policies you can purchase, including **dwelling, contents** and **personal liability.**

## Dwelling

House insurance covers damage or loss to the building you live in. It also covers the contents. Your policy will state which perils it covers and can include things like:

- **Fire**
- **Lightning**
- **Smoke** (not fireplaces)
- **Theft**
- **Water damage**
- **Wind**
- **Aircraft or vehicle impact**
- **Explosion**
- **Falling objects** (not caused by earthquake or snow slide)

> **Note:** check your policy carefully to see what is covered and what is not. Definitions may also vary. In general, the better your coverage, the higher will be your premium.

## Contents

This covers your possessions in the case of theft, damage or vandalism. Contents covered will usually include art, bicycles, boats, clothing, electronics, furniture, furnishings, jewellery, sports equipment and toys. Coverage limits on specific items vary, so shop around for a policy that suits your needs.

> **Note:** Keep your receipts in a safe place, as you'll be asked to provide receipts and appraisals for valuable items. This will include model and serial numbers where applicable. It's recommended that you provide photos/video of the contents of your home.

## Personal liability

This covers you for legal and medical costs when someone is injured on your property. It will also cover condo owners if your pipes leak and cause damage to another unit. The amount and type of coverage may vary from company to company and will affect your premiums.

## Uninsured activities

These exclusions are risks that are not covered in standard home policies and include:

- **home-sharing activities** like Airbnb.
- **criminal activities** of any kind
- **moral risk**
- **business use**

## Optional coverages

Common disaster coverage you may have to purchase separately:

- **Flood**

- **Windstorm**

- **Earthquake**

- **Sewer Back-up**

- **Equipment Breakdown**: covers unforeseen breakdowns in equipment like washers, dryers, stoves, fridges, dishwashers, furnaces, air conditioners, security systems and computers.

- **Guaranteed Replacement Cost**: provides the actual amount needed to repair your home or replace contents.

- **Personal Articles** like jewellery, electronics, fine art, collectables, bikes or boats may not be fully protected.

> **Note:** An Umbrella policy can cover expenses outside the limits of your other policies.

## Activities that can void your coverage

- Renovations can change the value and risk of your house. Remember to update your policy, so you don't have any unpleasant surprises.

- Extended periods of time away from your home without someone checking on your house.

- Not maintaining your house.

- Starting or running a home business

> **Note:** Promptly inform your insurer of any changes to your home or contents. As a rule of thumb, the better the information your insurer has, the better will be your coverage.

## Term Life Insurance

### What is Term Life Insurance?

This type of insurance guarantees payment of a specific death benefit on the death of the insured during a specified term. At the end of the term, the policyholder can either renew it for another term at increased cost, convert the policy to permanent coverage, or allow the policy to terminate. It has no savings component or cash value other than the death benefit. It is less expensive than an equivalent permanent life insurance policy. Premiums are based on your age, health and life expectancy, as set by the insurer. Other factors often considered are your smoking status, occupation, hobbies and family history. A medical exam may be required.

### Types of Term Life Insurance

### 1. Level term or level-premium policies

Coverage is provided for a specific period from 5 to 30 years. Many of the lower term policies are renewable without evidence of insurability for an increased premium. Your death benefit and the premium are otherwise fixed. Because the insurer is responsible for the increasing costs of insurance over each term of the policy, the premium is more expensive than yearly renewable term (YRT) life insurance. These policies are usually convertible to permanent policies prior to expiry, which is a great benefit should you become uninsurable during the life of the policy.

## 2. YRT policies

Coverage is renewable every year without requiring evidence of insurability. At first, premiums are low, but as you age premiums increase, which can make them prohibitively expensive.

## 3. Decreasing term policies

The death benefit declines each year according to a schedule determined by the insurer. You pay a fixed or level premium for the length of the policy. Decreasing term policies are commonly used to cover the declining principal of mortgages.

## Who Will Benefit from Term Life?

Term life is mostly used to insure young couples with children. They can obtain large amounts of coverage for reasonably low costs. Upon the death of a parent, the benefit can be used to replace lost income. Other uses are for Key Person insurance in businesses or to cover off temporary loans.

## Term Life vs Permanent Insurance

The choice between a cash-value permanent policy (whole life or universal life) and term life depends on your needs.

## Cost of Premiums

Term life policies are intended for people who want a large death benefit at a low cost. The policies are not usually sustainable for life because of ever-increasing premiums. You may pay more in premiums for less coverage when buying permanent life, but you have the security of knowing you're protected for life. And, in the long run, premiums may end up being less expensive for permanent life policies.

## Investment Value

Permanent life insurance usually has an investment or savings vehicle. Part of each of your premiums is allocated to that cash value. Some plans even pay dividends. These can be paid out or rolled into the cash value. Over time, cash value growth may become large enough to maintain the premiums on the policy without further investment by you. There are also tax benefits, like tax-deferred cash value growth and tax-free access to that money.

Other investments can usually beat the rate of return within a permanent policy. However, the functions of the vehicles are completely different.

> **Note:** In the end, your needs will determine whether you buy term and invest the difference or choose a permanent policy.

## Types of Permanent Insurance

*Universal life* and *whole life* are the most common types of permanent life insurance. Whole life protects your interests for your lifetime, and its cash value can grow at a guaranteed rate. Universal life is a type of insurance in which the payments of the insured are placed in an investment fund, earnings from which pay the premium on term life insurance while any remainder continues to increase the policy's value. Note: after an accumulation period, you can borrow from the cash values of each type of policy or use the cash value to pay the premiums of the policy.

> **Important note:** If the amount of the loan and unpaid interest ever exceeds the policy's cash value, the insurance policy will terminate, and your coverage will be lost.

## Critical Illness Insurance

This is an insurance product where the insurer is usually contracted to make a lump sum cash payment if he or she is diagnosed with or treated for one of the illnesses listed on the policy.

There may be certain qualifiers in your policy, like a survival period that must first be met or a surgical procedure like heart by-pass surgery. In other words, not all policies are created equal. The basic structure of critical illness insurance tends to be five-year renewable terms.

## Disability Insurance

Disability insurance protects you from an unexpected illness or accident that leaves you unable to work and earn an income.

Generally, this type of insurance replaces between 55% and 85% of your regular income, up to a maximum amount, for a specified time provided you:

- temporarily can't work
- become permanently disabled

> **Note:** Permanent refers to the nature of the disability. It doesn't mean you'll get benefits for the rest of your life. Policies of this nature usually terminate after a set period like two years or five years or at age 65.

Many employers carry disability insurance as part of their group plans. You can, however, secure your own policy through a life insurance professional. And, if you're self-employed, you can get disability insurance that will cover many of your business expenses should you be unable to work.

## Short-term Insurance

Short-term disability coverage pays benefits from periods of two weeks up to six months while you're sick or injured.

Should you or your employer not have a short-term disability plan, you can file for EI (Employment Insurance) sickness benefits. To be eligible for these, you must have used all of your sick leave and have worked enough hours to qualify for the benefits.

## Long-term Insurance

Long-term disability coverage generally begins when short-term disability insurance ends, you've used up any sick leave benefits from your employer, and when EI benefits have been exhausted.

## Definition of Disability

The definition of a disability often varies between plans and insurers. The definitions used are as follows:

## Any occupation

You'll receive disability benefits only if you can't perform the duties of any job for which you're reasonably suited.

## Regular or own occupation

You'll receive benefits if you're unable to perform the main duties of the job you had at the time the disability started.

> **Note:** Own occupation policies will often change to any occupation after the first two or five years. This is because own occupation policies tend to cost more than any occupation plans.

## Other sources of disability benefits

Disability benefits are also available from the Canada Pension Plan (CPP) and the Quebec Pension Plan (QPP). These benefits will pay if you have contributed to either of the plans and meet the any occupation disability definition, as set out by the government.

> **Note:** Your benefits from group or individual disability plan and the CPP or QPP will not exceed the 55-85 % threshold of your regular pay. Therefore, one or the other will be reduced to respect this threshold.

## Disability Insurance Benefits and Taxes

If you pay the entire amount of your premium, your disability benefits will be tax-free. If your employer pays any part of the premium, your disability benefits will be taxed at your personal rate.

**Note:** There are many definitions and rules that apply to disability insurance. Make sure you read your personal or group plan and ask questions about anything you don't understand.

Insurance can be a complicated issue: for a complimentary needs analysis or to get your questions answered, contact Thomas Hurley at **tombhur@gmail.com**.

## Notes

_____

_____

_____

_____

_____

_____

_____

_____

_____

_____

_____

_____

_____

_____

_____

_____

_____

_____

_____

_____

_____

_____

_____

## *Notes*

# Chapter 4

# Mutual Funds, Annuities and Mortgages

**M**utual funds are an investment vehicle you can purchase to help with your financial future. They consist of stocks, bonds, cash and other financial vehicles like debentures. Some advantages are that they are managed by professionals daily or sometimes even hourly. Most mutual funds have relatively low management fees, even though the management people decide when to buy and sell each investment vehicle. Stocks may go up, and the management people will decide when to sell if they think they will be going down in value.

Mutual funds can be part of other financial strategies. One of them is holding them inside your RRSP (Registered Retirement Saving Plan) if you qualify. You can put up to 18% of your income into RRSPs, and it says on your notice of assessment how much that will be in the following year. One advantage of RRSPs is that you can deduct the amount you deposit in a year and even 60 days past the end of the year into an RRSP from your taxable income. This is based on the premise that you're in a high tax bracket, and when you retire, you'll be in a lower tax bracket. These financial instruments in your RRSP grow tax-exempt until you take the money out of your RRSP. You can contribute to your RRSP until you turn 71 at which time you have to close the RRSP, or you can roll the money over to RRIF (Registered Retirement Income Fund), which I will explain later. This rollover keeps the money tax-free until you take the money out. You can also deposit cash to a spousal RRSP which gives the money to your spouse, and when they take the money out at retirement, it may be at a lower tax rate. You cannot deposit above your limit for any particular year without a penalty.

**Segregated funds** are sold by life insurance companies. They're insurance contracts that invest in one or more underlying assets (a mutual fund, for example).

Segregated funds are different from mutual funds; they provide a guarantee to protect 75% to 100% of the money you invest. In other words, if the underlying fund loses money, the life insurance company guarantees to return some or all of your principal investment. However, you must hold your investment for a certain length of time (usually ten years) to benefit from the guarantee. You also pay a fee for this insurance protection. **Warning:** should you cash out before the maturity date of the segregated fund, the guarantee won't apply. You'll be paid the current market value of your investment, minus any fees you agreed to pay. This dollar amount may be more or less than what you originally invested.

## Three advantages of segregated funds:

1. **Your principal is guaranteed**—Depending on the insurance contract, 75% to 100% of your initial investment is guaranteed. You must, as mentioned, hold your fund for a certain length of time (usually ten years). Should the value of the underlying investment rise, some segregated funds also let you "reset" the guaranteed amount to this higher value. Note: resetting the fund also extends the length of time you must hold the fund (usually ten years from the date of reset).

2. There's **a guaranteed death benefit**—Your beneficiaries will receive 75% to 100% of your contributions tax-free when you die (depending on the contract). This amount won't be subject to probate fees as long as your beneficiaries are named in the contract.

3. **Potential creditor protection**—This is a feature meant for business owners in particular.

## Three disadvantages of segregated funds:

1. **Your money is locked in**—To get the principal guarantee, you must keep your money in the fund until the maturity date to get the guarantee. Otherwise, all you'll get is the current market value of your investment, which may be more or less than what you originally invested.

2. **Higher fees**—Segregated funds often have higher Management Expense Ratios (MERs) than mutual funds. This covers the cost of the insurance features.

3. **Penalties for early withdrawals**—If you cash out before the maturity date, the company may charge you a penalty.

## Individual (retail) versus group retirement plan segregated funds

If you have a workplace pension or savings plan that's administered by an insurance company, the fund options available to you will typically be segregated funds. However, these group segregated funds don't carry the insurance guarantee and higher fees associated with segregated funds you buy as an individual. Because they're insurance contracts, group segregated funds do offer creditor protection and the avoidance of probate fees if a beneficiary is named.

A **TFSA (Tax-Free Savings Account)** is another strategy for saving money. In this account, you can currently put up to 65,000 dollars, and the money will grow tax-free. One of the advantages of this account is that you can withdraw the funds without a tax liability. Once you open a TFSA, you can deposit money anytime, up to your limit. The purpose of this account is to get people saving money. The money you deposit in a TFSA is not tax-deductible.

An **RRIF (Registered Retirement Income Fund)** is another investment strategy to help people in retirement. When you turn 71, you have to cash in your RRSP, or you can roll it into an RRIF. This rollover can occur before you're 71. With money in a RRIF, a person has to withdraw so much a year as designated by government regulations. With this strategy, you should be retired and in a lower tax bracket than when you were working. If the money put into the RRIF is from a spousal RRSP, then the money goes into a spousal RRIF and may be taxed at a lower rate than it would have been in the primary contributor's tax. You can withdraw more than the minimum but not less. As with most strategies, I would suggest you engage a professional to help you.

An **RDSP (Registered Disability Saving Plan)** is a plan to help parents and others save for the long-term financial security of a disabled person. A person must be eligible for the disability tax credit (DTC) which is a form filed with the government and completed by a doctor. The contributions are not tax-deductible and must occur by the end of the year in which the beneficiary turns 59. Contributions can be made by the parents or anyone else, including a grant by the government which needs to be applied for.

An **RESP (Registered Education Saving Plan)** is a plan to save for your children's postsecondary education. It's a way to empower power your child to ensure there are no limits on their dreams as there will be money available. You can open a plan for your child or your grandchild. The earlier you start an RESP the better. If your child is a bit older, don't worry about getting started as it can help your child take advantage of government grants if the child is 15 years or older. You can contribute to a maximum of $50,000 per child over the life of the plan. Generally, it's a good idea to contribute monthly or annually. Your contributions will be matched by the federal government up to 20% or $500 annually, assuming there is no carry forward room in any given year. The lifetime maximum for government contributions is $7200. An RESP can stay open for up to 36 years, so the child has a long time to decide if they want postsecondary education.

**Annuities** are primarily a retirement strategy and have several phases. An annuity is a financial product that pays a fixed sum of money to someone each year, typically for the rest of their life. The accumulation phase is when the annuity is being funded before the annuitization stage. An annuity can be funded in many ways. One way is by converting an RRSP or RRIF into an annuity. Also, there can be lump sum payments into the annuity, such as the sale of a business which may generate a large amount of cash that could fund the annuity. The annuitization can be structured with different kinds of instruments. These instruments can be fixed, variable, immediate or deferred income to give the investor flexibility in their financial strategies. These annuities are designed to be a reliable means of securing steady cash flow for an individual during their retirement years, to remove the fear of outliving one's assets. They can also be created to turn a substantial lump sum into a steady cash flow. Defined benefit pensions and social security are two examples of lifetime guaranteed annuities that pay retirees a steady stream of cash until they pass. They can also be structured to pay out a spouse with a survivor benefit. The annuity can begin with immediate payment, or it can be deferred to a specific age or date that one would like. The annuities can also be fixed or variable. Fixed annuities provide a regular periodic payment whereas variable annuities allow the owner to receive more significant future cash flows if investments in the annuity fund do well, or smaller payments if its investments do poorly.

**Exchange-traded funds (ETF)** are mutual funds that an investor can buy and sell over the internet. ETF funds may have generally lower expense ratios than actively traded mutual funds. These funds can contain all types of investments, including stocks, commodities or bonds, and some offer US investments. ETF funds are used by day traders and others who want to buy and sell stocks every day. Sometimes regular traders use them as well.

With these different strategies, it's up to the individual to do their homework and seek the advice of experienced advisors. An RRSP is similar to a 401K plan in the US. In both countries, it's necessary to find a qualified tax accountant.

**Reverse mortgages** are mortgages only property owners who have sufficient equity in their property can qualify for. If you own a house with 50% equity, then you may be eligible for a mortgage with no payment, and you'll be able to stay in the house with little or no payments until you sell or die. The exact details have to be worked out with the mortgage company.

Investing on your mind? Thomas can help. Contact him at **tombhur@gmail.com**.

## Notes

_____

_____

_____

_____

_____

_____

_____

_____

_____

_____

_____

_____

_____

_____

_____

_____

_____

_____

_____

## Notes

_____

_____

_____

_____

_____

_____

_____

_____

_____

_____

_____

_____

_____

_____

_____

_____

_____

_____

_____

# Chapter 5

# Stock Exchanges

## Stock Exchanges

The primary function of a Stock Exchange is to help provide liquidity. In other words, it gives the sellers a place to sell and buyers to buy shareholdings. Another purpose is for a company to conduct its initial public offering (IPO), where a company sells shares to an initial set of public shareholders. After the IPO floats shares into the hands of public shareholders, these shares can be sold and purchased on an exchange. The exchange facilitates the buying and selling of stocks as well as tracking the buy and sell price and the volume turnover. You need an account to buy and sell stocks on an exchange. Sixteen stock exchanges in the world sell over US 1 trillion dollars each. We'll only be discussing a few of them in this book. A list of the stock exchanges and their hours can be found on **https: // www.trading hours. com/exchanges**.

**NYSE** is The New York Stock Exchange and is the largest and most prestigious exchange. This exchange is located in New York City. Listing on NYSE gives companies credibility because they must meet the initial listing requirements and also comply annually with maintenance requirements. For US companies to remain listed, they must keep their price share above $4 per share and their market capitalization, which is the number of shares times price, above 40 million dollars. The investors trading on the NYSE benefit from a set of minimum protections. For example, the companies must get shareholder approval for any equity incentive plan. In the past, companies were allowed to sidestep shareholder approval if their equity incentive plan met specific criteria. However, this prevented shareholders from knowing how many stock options were available for future grants. Secondly, the majority of the board of directors must be independent. However, each company has some discretion over the term "independent" which causes some controversy.

**NASDAQ** is an acronym for the National Association of Security Dealers Automated Quotations. It's located in New York City. In 1971 NASDAQ began operations as the world's first electronic stock market. The NASDAQ helped lower the bid-ask spread, which is the difference between the bid price and ask price of the stock. NASDAQ eventually assumed the majority of trades that had been executed by over-the-counter (OTC) system of trading. As late as 1987 the NASDAQ was commonly referred to as OTC in media reports. From 1981 to 1991 NASDAQ moved from 37% to 46% of the total securities sold in the US. In 1992 NASDAQ joined with the London Stock Exchange to form the first intercontinental linkage of capital markets.

The **TSX** (Toronto Stock Exchange) is located in Toronto, Ontario, Canada and was formed in 1852 by Toronto businessmen with intentions of creating an association of brokers. By 1901 the TSX had risen to 100 companies in an annual trading volume of close to a million shares. In 1914 concerns about financial panic due to World War One prompted the shutdown of the TSX for three months. By 1929 trading had risen to over 10,000,000 shares but the boom times ended with the Great Depression of the 1930s. In 1936 the TSX had become North America's 3rd largest exchange with annual trading volume exceeding 500 million. The S&P/TSX (Standard and Poors/Toronto Stock Exchange) Composite index represents roughly 70% of the total market capitalization on the TSX, with about 250 companies included in it. The TSX is made up of over 1500 companies.

There are over 150 stock exchanges in the world. You can find stock exchanges in several languages such as Chinese, Japanese, German, and in different currencies.

## Buying and Selling Stocks

To buy stocks, you need a stockbroker. The reason for this is you usually can't call up a company and ask to buy their stock on your own. If you're an inexperienced investor, there are two categories of brokers you can access: a full-service broker or an online/discount broker.

## Full-Service Brokers

Full-service brokers are traditional stockbrokers who'll take the time to get to know you personally and financially. They'll consider factors like age (time horizon), assets, debts, income, lifestyle, marital status, personality, risk tolerance and more. Your broker can then help you develop a long-term financial plan.

Not only can your broker help you with your investment needs, he or she can also provide budgeting, estate planning, retirement planning, tax advice, etcetera, hence the term "full-service." Such a broker can help you manage all of your financial needs now and long into the future and is for an investor who wants everything in one package.

Naturally, the value in having a professional investment advisor can be well worth any additional costs.

You can open a full-service broker account with as little as $1,000.

## Online/Discount Brokers

Online/discount brokers don't provide any investment advice and are just order takers. They're much less expensive than full-service brokers since there's typically no office to visit and no certified investment advisor(s) to help you. Cost is generally based on a per-transaction basis, and you can open an account over the internet with little or no money. Once you have secured account with an online broker, you can go to their website, log into your account and begin buying and selling stocks instantly.

**Warning:** these types of brokers provide no investment advice, stock tips or any kind of investment help. It's up to you to manage your investments. The only assistance you'll receive is technical support; you should be able to find investment-related links, research and resources that can be useful.

This discussion can help you understand that your choice of broker should be based on your individual needs. Full-service brokers work with those who will pay a premium for someone else to look after their finances. Conversely, online/discount brokers are perfect for people with little start-up money and who are willing to take upon themselves the risks (and rewards) of investing.

## Direct Stock Purchase Plan

Sometimes, companies (often blue-chip firms) will sponsor an investment program called a DSPP, or Direct Stock Purchase Plan. DSPPs are a way for businesses to let smaller investors acquire ownership directly from the company. To start a DSPP, you communicate with a company rather than a broker. However, each company's system for administering a DSPP is unique, although many offer their DSPP through transfer agents or another third-party administrator. To learn more about a specific company's DSPP, you should contact the company's investor relations department.

As mentioned, you can buy or sell stock on your own by opening a brokerage account. What you do is connect it with your bank chequing account to make deposits, which are then available for you to invest.

**Warning**: it's recommended that beginners speak to a qualified financial advisor. New investors should also read *The Intelligent Investor* by Benjamin Graham.

## The Basics of Buying and Selling Stocks

Before you begin to buy and sell stocks, you need to know the different types of orders and when using them is appropriate. They are as follows:

- A market order is used for buying or selling shares at the prevailing market prices until the order is filled.

- A limit order determines a share price at which a trade must be initiated. However, there's no guarantee that the order will trade—if, for example, the limit is set too high or low.

- Stop orders are a type of limit order and are triggered when a stock moves above or below a certain level. They're primarily used as a way to insure against significant losses or to lock in profits.

## Market Order Versus Limit Order

A **market order** is how you buy or sell immediately at the current price. Typically, if you're going to buy a stock, then you'll pay a price at or near the posted ask. If you're going to sell a stock, you'll receive a price at or near the posted bid.

Something you need to understand is that the last traded price isn't guaranteed to be the price at which the market order will be filled. When the market is volatile, the price at which you execute the trade can be quite different from the last traded price. The price will be the same only when the bid and ask prices are identical to the last traded price. Note: market orders on stocks that trade over tens of thousands of shares per day will be more likely to execute close to the actual bid and ask prices.

A **limit order**, or pending order, allows you to buy and sell at a specific price in the future. It's used to execute a trade if the price reaches a pre-defined level; the order won't be filled if the price doesn't reach this level. So, a limit order sets the maximum or minimum price at which you're willing to buy or sell a stock.

For example, if a particular stock was $15, you could enter a limit order for this amount. This means that you wouldn't pay a penny over $15 for that particular stock. However, it's still possible for you to buy it for less than the $15 per share specified in the order.

The four types of limit order are:

- **Buy Limit** is an order to purchase at or below a specified price. This means placing the buy limit order at or below the current market bid.

- **Sell Limit** is an order to sell at or above a certain price. To ensure improved price, you need to place the order at or above the current market ask.

- **Buy Stop** is an order to buy a stock at a price above the current market bid. A stop order is executed only after a specified price level is reached (known as the stop level). Once a stop level is reached, the order will be immediately converted into a market or limit order.

- **Sell Stop** is an order you place to sell at a price below the current market ask. The order is activated once the specified price is reached.

## Market and Limit Order Costs

When choosing a market or limit order, you should be aware of the costs. Generally, commissions are less for market orders than for limit orders. The difference can be anywhere from a couple of dollars to more than $10. For example, a $7 commission on a market order can be boosted up to $12 when you place a limit restriction. So, when you place a limit order, make sure it's worthwhile, that the math works. Also, in the case of the limit order, it's possible that the stock doesn't fall to the set price or less. In fact, if it continues to rise, you may lose the opportunity to buy.

> **Warning:** Knowing the difference between a limit and a market order is fundamental to individual investing. By understanding what each order does and how each one might affect your trading, you can identify which order suits your investment needs, saves you time, reduces your risk, and, most importantly, saves you money.

## *Additional Stock Order Types

- **Stop-loss Order** (also known as a stopped market, on-stop buy or on-stop sell): This order remains dormant until a fixed downside price is passed, at which time it's activated as a market order. Consider using this type of order when you don't have time to watch the market continually (e.g., when you go on vacation) but need protection from a significant downside move.

- **Stop-limit Order:** This one is complicated, as there are two prices specified. First, there's the stop price, which converts the order to a sell order. Then comes the limit price, where the order becomes one that will only execute at the limit price or better. The stop-limit order can correct a potential problem with stop-loss orders, which can be triggered during a flash crash when prices plummet but then subsequently recover.

- **All or None** (AON): This order is often used by those who buy penny stocks. An all-or-none order guarantees you get the entire quantity of stock you want (or none at all). For example, let's say you put in an order to buy 3,000 shares of ABC but only 1,500 are being sold, an all-or-none restriction means your order won't be filled until there are at least 3,000 shares available at your preferred price. This is important because if you don't place an all-or-none restriction, your 3,000 share order would be partially filled for 1,500 shares.

- **Immediate or Cancel** (IOC): This order ensures that whatever amount of an order can be placed (or at a limit) in a short period—often just a few seconds or less—is filled, then the rest of the order cancelled. If no shares are traded in the immediate interval, the order is cancelled.

- **Fill or Kill** (FOK) is an order that an AON order with an IOC specification. It requires that the entire order size be traded and in a short time period. Both conditions must be met or the order is cancelled.

- **Good 'Til Cancelled** (GTC): A good 'til cancelled order remains active until you decide to cancel it, within limits set by your brokerages (usually 90 days).

- **Day:** If you don't specify the time of expiry through a GTC, then your order will usually be set as a day order. This means the order will expire after the end of the trading day.

- **Take Profit:** Also referred to as a profit target, this order closes out the trade—at a profit—once it has reached a certain level. It's **always** connected to an open position of a pending order.

*\*Please note that not all brokerages or online trading platforms allow for all types of orders. Check with your broker if you don't have access to an order type you want to use.*

## *Notes*

_____

_____

_____

_____

_____

_____

_____

_____

_____

_____

_____

_____

_____

_____

_____

_____

_____

_____

_____

_____

_____

_____

# Chapter 6

# Commodities

ommodity trading is different from trading stocks and should only be attempted by an experienced trader. Stock companies also trade some commodities. There are several different sectors of commodities such as energy, metals and agriculture. One of the stock exchanges that handles commodities is the Chicago Stock Exchange (CHX), although there are others.

**The energy sector** has things like crude oil, natural gas and electricity. These types of commodities can change because of the political climate of the particular countries that are significant producers. For instance, with crude oil, the price has gone from about USD 160.00 a barrel to as low as USD 25.00 and today is approximately USD 62.00 a barrel. OPEC (Organization of Petroleum Exporting Countries) has some control over the supply and demand of crude oil. Still, the dumping of crude oil by countries like Saudi Arabia can change the price almost overnight. By comparison, natural gas and electricity are more stable because there is more of an abundance of them. Global demand and political and economic stability affect the price of these commodities. As the economy improves the demand increases, and as the economy has inflation, the demand decreases.

**Metals** include things like gold, silver, platinum and palladium, which are some of the precious metals. Aluminum and copper are more abundant but are only available in some parts of the world. Gold is usually used to set the value of the U.S. dollar as a benchmark for trading. The U.S. also uses gold as a hedge against inflation. Many of these metals are used in the production of hobby equipment, especially computers, TVs and associated equipment. The advent of the cell phone has increased the demand for lots of these metals.

When you think of **agriculture**, you may think of the greens that are grown in Canada and the U.S. but also includes things like coffee and other items from around the world. We get a lot of our fruit from countries like Mexico and New Zealand (one of the only places producing kiwi fruit). Agriculture also includes livestock such as cattle, hogs, sheep and the parts of these animals. Commodities like coffee are grown in Brazil and Africa, just as rubber is grown in some unique localities. These types of commodities are subject to weather and diseases that affect the crops. As with other commodities, agriculture prices fluctuate with supply and demand. Market volatility is a problem for farmers around the world.

All of these products are at high risk for volatility. Also, there's a problem with storage, security and control of shipping of such commodities. A lot of these commodities are perishable, so they have to be stored in the proper facilities. The products are checked before they leave the farms for the appropriate moisture content so that they may not be contaminated. Security is a problem because agricultural products are easily stolen or damaged.

Agricultural commodities are bought and sold on many exchanges around the world. They're also traded by exchange-traded funds (ETF). These products, because of their nature, take special storage and handling facilities, including large ocean-going ships to move them. Some agricultural commodities are bought as futures which means the price is set today for delivery of the goods in the future. Some of these products are purchased and have to be processed to be resold to the end consumer. An example is meat products where the animals are bought, processed and frozen before shipment to store suppliers.

Commodities are a significant part of our daily lives. Anyone who drives a car can be affected by rising crude oil prices. A drought that impacts the soybean supply may influence your next meal. Similarly, commodities can diversify an investment portfolio—

either for the long-term or to act as a vehicle for parking cash while the market is in turmoil (because commodities tend to move in opposition to stocks).

## Commodities Exchanges

The most popular exchanges in the U.S. are the CME Group (Chicago Mercantile Exchange), the Atlanta Intercontinental Exchange and the Kansas City Board of Trade.

## Commodities Market Characteristics

Economic principles of supply and demand tend to drive the commodities markets. The lower the supply, the higher the demand, which equals increased prices; the higher the supply, the lower the demand, which equals lower prices. An example of these principles would be a significant disruption in supply, like a widespread cattle health scare, which could lead to a spike in the generally stable and predictable demand for livestock. Another example is the emergence of China and India as significant manufacturing players, which has resulted in a decreasing supply of industrial metals, such as steel. This will, of course, put pressure on the market and increase prices.

## Types of Commodities

Today, tradable commodities fall into four categories:

- **Metals** (such as copper, gold, platinum and silver)

- **Energy** (such as crude oil, diesel, gasoline, heating oil and natural gas)

- **Livestock and Meat** (including feeder cattle, lean hogs, live cattle and pork bellies)

- **Agricultural** (including cocoa, coffee, corn, cotton, rice, soybeans, sugar and wheat)

Volatile or bearish stock markets often find investors scrambling to transfer money to commodities like gold, which has historically presented as a reliable, dependable metal with transferable value. Precious metals are also used as a hedge against increasing inflation or periods of declining currency value.

Increasing energy demands, economic downturns, production changes by OPEC and emerging technological advances (such as wind, solar and biofuel) will affect crude oil demand and, thus, prices.

The agricultural market (grains, etcetera) can be volatile during summer months or periods of weather transitions. Another example is population growth and limited supply increasing agricultural prices.

## Investing in Commodities Through Futures

A way to invest in commodities is through an agreement to buy or sell a specific quantity of product at a set price at a later time (a futures contract).

## Who Uses Futures Contracts

Two types of investors use the futures markets: actual commercial or institutional **users** of the commodities and speculators. Manufacturers and service providers use futures contracts as a way to budget expenses and minimize cash flow problems. They do this by taking a position that will reduce the risk of financial loss due to changing prices. For example, the airline industry must secure vast quantities of fuel at stable prices as part of its planning process. Using futures contracts, airlines buy fuel at fixed rates for a period of time to flatten the effect of market volatility in crude oil and gasoline. This makes their financial statements less volatile and risky for investors. Speculators buy similar contracts but typically close out their positions before the contract is due and never take delivery of the grain, oil and such.

## How to Trade Futures

You must have a stockbroker who also trades futures. You'll be asked to complete a form indicating you understand the risks associated with commodity trading.

Each contract requires a different minimum deposit. If the value of the contract decreases, you'll receive a margin call and will have to deposit more money into your account to keep the position open. Due to the massive amounts of leverage involved in contract trading, small price movements can result in a futures account being extinguished or doubled in a few minutes.

## The Advantages of Futures:

- Leverage allows for big profits if you're on the right side of the trade

- Minimum-deposit accounts control entire contracts that you would otherwise not be able to afford

- You can go long or short with ease

## The Disadvantages of Futures:

- Futures markets can be unbelievably volatile, and direct investment can be precarious—especially for inexperienced investors

- Leverage magnifies both your gains and losses

- You could lose your deposit (and more) before you're able to close your position

---

**Note:** Most futures contracts will have options associated with them. Buying options on futures contracts is much like putting a deposit on something rather than purchasing it; you have the right, but not the obligation, to follow through on the transaction. In other words, if the price of the contract doesn't move in the direction you anticipated, you won't lose more than the cost of the option.

---

### Advantages of Stock Options:

- Investors will usually have a brokerage account

- Public information on a company's financial situation is available

- Many times, the stocks are highly liquid

### Disadvantages of Stock Options:

- A stock isn't a pure play on commodity prices

- The option price can be influenced by specific company factors as well as market conditions

### ETFs and ETNs

Exchange traded funds (ETFs) or exchange-traded notes (ETNs) trade like stocks, allowing investors to access commodity price fluctuations without purchasing futures contracts.

Commodity **ETFs** generally track the price of a commodity

or group of commodities in a particular index by using futures contracts. However, some investors will back the ETF with the real commodity that's held in storage.

**ETNs** are unsecured debt that mimics the price changes of a commodity or commodity index and are backed by the issuer. A special brokerage account isn't needed to invest in ETFs or ETNs.

## Advantages of ETFs and ETNs:

- No management or redemption fees because they trade like stocks

- An easy way to access the price fluctuation of a commodity or group of commodities

## Disadvantages of ETFs and ETNs:

- A big move in the commodity might not be reflected accurately by the underlying ETF or ETN

- Not all commodities are associated with an ETF or ETN

- ETNs represent a credit risk

## Investing in Commodities Using Mutual and Index Funds

Mutual funds can't invest directly in commodities. However, they can invest in the stocks of companies involved in commodity-related industries (e.g. energy, agriculture or mining). The fund shares can be affected by factors other than commodity prices, including stock market fluctuations and company-specific risks.

Some commodity index mutual funds invest in futures contracts and commodity-linked derivative investments. This provides more direct exposure to commodity prices.

**Advantages of Commodity Mutual and Index Funds:**

- Enjoy professional money management

- More diversification

- Better liquidity

**Disadvantages of Commodity Mutual and Index Funds:**

- Higher management fees

- Some funds may have sale charges

- They aren't a pure play on commodity prices

## Commodity Pool Operators and Trading Advisors

A commodity pool operator (CPO) (person or limited partnership) gathers money from investors and invests it in futures contracts and options. CPOs must provide a risk disclosure document to investors, distribute periodic account statements and issue annual financial reports. They're also required to keep strict records of all investors, transactions and pools they operate.

CPOs use commodity trading advisors (CTAs) to advise them. CTAs have to register with the Commodity Futures Trading Commission (CFTC). They're also required to undergo an FBI background check before being allowed to give investment advice.

**Advantages of CTAs:**

- Provide professional advice

- Pools provide more money for a CPO to invest

- Closed fund structure requires all individuals to invest the same amount of money

## Disadvantages of CTAs:

- May be difficult to evaluate past performance

- The trading program may be susceptible to drawdowns (a peak-to-trough decline during a specific period for an investment, fund, or trading account)

**Final Note:** Commodities can rapidly become risky investments because they can be affected by such factors as unusual weather patterns, epidemics and natural disasters.

## Notes

_____

_____

_____

_____

_____

_____

_____

_____

_____

_____

_____

_____

_____

_____

_____

_____

_____

_____

_____

_____

# Chapter 7

# Day Trading

Day trading is a financial/investment strategy that requires a lot of knowledge and education about stocks and bonds. Speed of trades, reliability, and low cost are some of the reasons people day trade.

Investopedia is an excellent resource for getting knowledge, a dictionary of terms, stock simulators and other help. There are many more online courses and webinars for help. These online resources also contain many algorithms for picking stocks.

Most day traders open with no trades active and close all trades before the end of the day because stocks may close the day at one price and open the next day at a different price. It's necessary that you use charts for comparison of the rise and fall of prices. You also need a list of acronyms as learning the language is so important. Some terms you need to know as a start for your list are: fundamentals, volume, volatility, charts, strategy, index and many abbreviations. By googling stock market abbreviations, you can come up with a substantial list as well as getting a description of any terms you may not understand. Educating yourself is vitally important. There are many tutorials on the internet.

Fees can go as low as $0.005 per share with a minimum of $1.00 per trade. Every brokerage has a different fee schedule. Day trading usually works with the purchase and sale of a volume of shares, and you're looking for stocks with a high volume of sales, so you have no problem selling your shares before the end of the day. The study of various strategies, especially for new traders, is essential. Different commodities require different strategies. If you pick the right brokers, they may offer tutorials at no cost so you may practice trading without losing money to get the experience.

Most brokerages require you have $25,000 or more in your account before you start day trading.

## Trading Tips for the Beginner

Small price moves can bring you significant profits—if you play the game correctly. But it can be dangerous for anyone who doesn't adhere to a solid strategy. Also, consider the fact that not all brokers are suitable for placing high volume trades. Some of the best brokers for the day trader are Interactive Brokers, Lightspeed, Tastyworks, TD Ameritrade and Tradestation.

These brokers typically offer advanced platforms featuring charting tools, real-time streaming quotes and the ability to enter and modify complex orders quickly.

> **Please note** that day trading is only profitable when you take it seriously and do your research. It's a job, not a hobby—be diligent, focused, objective, and detach your emotions.

## Strategies That Work

### 1. Information is power

Besides knowledge of basic trading procedures, day traders need to gather information regarding the latest stock market news and events that affect stocks—interest rates, economic outlook, and so on. So, do your homework. Make a list of the stocks you'd like to trade and keep yourself informed about those companies, as well as the market in general. Track business news and trustworthy financial websites.

## 2. Set aside some of your capital

What percentage of your funds are you willing to risk per trade? Successful day traders tend to risk less than 1% to 2% of their account on each trade. So, if you have $25,000 (the minimum day trading companies usually ask for) in your account and you're willing to risk 0.5% of your capital on each trade, your maximum loss per trade is $125 (0.005 x $25,000). **Note:** this approach requires that you set aside funds you can trade with that you're prepared to lose at any given time.

## 3. Make sure you have ample time

Day trading requires a lot of time (that's why it's called day trading). Don't do it if you can't commit most of your day. The process requires tracking of the markets to spot opportunities, which can arise at any time during trading hours. Making your move quickly is critical.

## 4. Start slowly and small

Focus on just one or two stocks each session. As it has become increasingly common to trade fractional shares (less than one full share of equity), you can invest smaller dollar amounts. For example, if a company's shares are trading at $200 and you only want to buy $40 worth, many brokers will now let you invest in a one-fifth share.

## 5. Avoid penny stocks

Penny stock refers to small company stocks that typically trade for less than $5 per share. Although some penny stocks trade on large exchanges such as the New York Stock Exchange (NYSE), you must purchase most of them over the counter (OTC). These stocks are often illiquid, and the chance of making a profit isn't good. As a beginner, you should simply stay away.

### 6. Time your trades

Many investors execute trades as soon as the markets open in the morning, which contributes to price volatility. It's good practice to just study the market without making any moves for the first 15 to 20 minutes. Movement also begins to pick up again toward the closing bell. Though these rush hours offer opportunities, it's safer for new day traders to avoid them.

### 7. Use limit orders to reduce losses

A limit order will guarantee the price but not the execution. You set an executable price for buying as well as selling. This helps you trade with more precision. More experienced day traders will also use options strategies to hedge their positions as well.

### 8. Be realistic regarding profits

Consider that many traders successfully conclude only 50% to 60% of their trades. The key is that they profit more from their winners than they lose on their losers. You must ensure the risk of loss on each trade is kept to a precise percentage of your account, and that your entry and exit methods are well defined and written down.

### 9. Manage your emotions

The stock market will surely test your nerves. You must learn to keep fear, greed and hope at bay. Govern your decisions with logic and not emotion.

## 10. Stick to your plan

As a day trader, you need to be prepared to move fast. It's therefore crucial that you develop a trading strategy **in advance**. It's equally important to have the discipline to stick to your plan rather than trying to chase profits.

## Why is Day Trading so Difficult?

Day trading is a skill you must acquire, and there's lots of information to gather. Here are a couple of things to consider: You're going up against professionals. They have access to top-tier technology and know all the right people, so they're positioned succeed. Your appearance in the fray just means higher profits for them. And don't forget the taxes. You'll pay on any short-term gains at the marginal rate. This includes investments held for less than one year. Happily, your losses help to offset any gains.

## How to Decide What and When You Buy

Day traders make money by successfully exploiting tiny price movements in specific assets (currencies, futures, options and stocks), usually using large amounts of borrowed capital to do so.

Three things should influence your focus:

- **Liquidity** is defined as how easily an asset or security can be converted to cash (buying or selling the asset at a price that reflects its actual value).

- **Volatility** is a measure of the expected daily price range in which you operate. High volatility equates to greater profit or loss.

- **Trading volume** is concerned with how many times a stock is bought and sold in a given time period. It's also referred to as the **average daily trading volume**. High volume indicates much interest in a stock and often foreshadows a price jump, either up or down.

Places you can garner this information from are:

- **Real-time news services:** News moves stocks, so subscribe to an excellent news service.

- **ECN/Level 2 quotes:** Electronic Communication Networks give you the best available bid and ask quotes on the market, then automatically match and execute your orders. Level 2 quotes provide real-time access to the Nasdaq order book.

- **Intraday candlestick charts:** Candlesticks provide a fundamental analysis of asset price action (more on these later).

First, define and write down the specific conditions under which you'll enter a position. Then, scan through candlestick charts to see if those conditions are generated for each period in which you're interested. If so, you have a *possible* entry point. The next step is to assess how to exit those trades.

## Creating an Exit Strategy

Profit targets (a predetermined point at which you'll exit a trade in a profitable position) are the most common method for selling an asset that's in a winning position. Note: your exit criteria must be specific enough to be repeatable and testable. Example price target strategies are:

## Scalping

Scalping involves selling almost immediately after a trade becomes profitable.

## Fading

Fading involves shorting stocks (betting on their decline) after rapid moves upward. This strategy is based on several assumptions: (1) the asset has been overbought, (2) early buyers are ready to sell and (3) current buyers may be scared away. Your price target will be when buyers begin to return.

## Daily Pivots

You buy at the low of the day and sell at the high of the day. (Of course, this is easier said than done!) The price target becomes the next sign of a reversal.

## Momentum

This strategy is about day trading based on news releases or finding strong trending moves supported by high volume. One trader might buy on news releases and ride a trend until it exhibits signs of reversal. Another may fade the price surge.

## Charts and Patterns

To help determine when to buy an asset, many traders use:

*__Candlestick patterns__, including Engulfing Candles and Dojis (A Doji forms when the opening price and the closing price are equal). The Doji represents indecision in the markets.

## Engulfing Candlestick Pattern

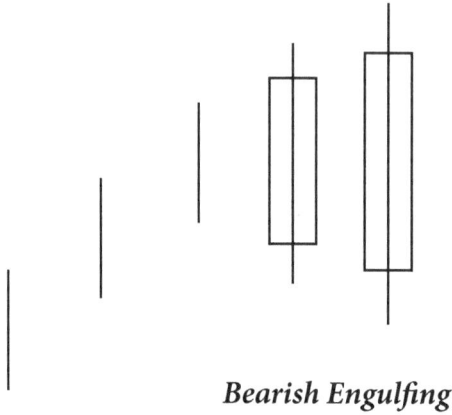

*Bearish Engulfing*

*It's a Bearish engulfing pattern because the second candle has engulfed the previous candle.*

## Gravestone Doji

High Price

Open & Close Price

Low Price

## Long-legged Doji

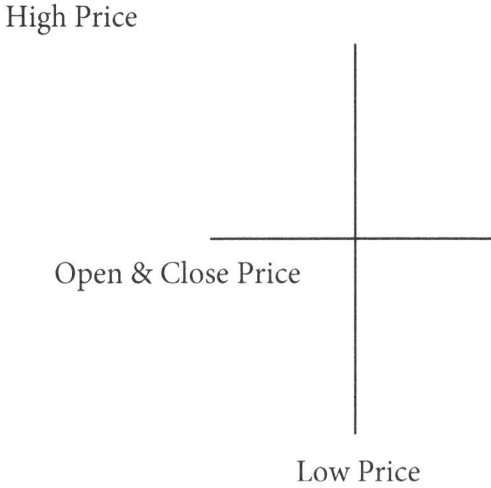

High Price

Open & Close Price

Low Price

## Death Cross Doji

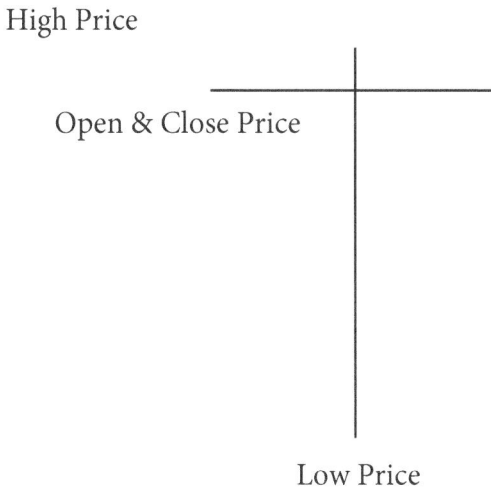

High Price

Open & Close Price

Low Price

* **Technical analysis**, including trend lines and triangles

**Ascending Triangle**     **Descending Triangle**

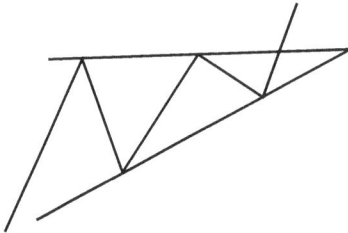

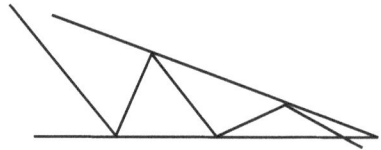

* **Volume**—increasing or decreasing

There are many candlestick setups a day trader can look for to find an entry point. If used properly, the doji reversal pattern is one of the most reliable ones.

Typically, look for a pattern like this with several confirmations:

1. First, look for a volume spike, which will show you whether traders are supporting the price at this level. Note: this can be either on the doji candle or on the candles immediately following it.

2. Second, look for prior support at this price level. For example, the prior low of day (LOD) or high of day (HOD).

3. Finally, look at the Level 2 situation, which will show all the open orders and order sizes.

If you follow these three steps, you can determine whether the doji is likely to produce an actual turnaround and can take a position if the conditions are favourable. Traditional analysis of chart patterns also provides profit targets for exits. For example, the height of a triangle at the widest part is added to the breakout point of the triangle (for an upside breakout), providing a price at which to take profits.

## How to Limit Your Losses

A stop-loss order limits losses on a position you've taken in a security. For a long position, place your stop-loss below a recent low; for short positions place the order above a recent high. You can also make your choice because of volatility. For example, if a stock price moves at about $0.1 a minute, then you might place a stop-loss $0.3 away from your entry. This gives the price room to fluctuate before it moves in the expected direction.

The point, of course, is to define precisely how you'll control the risk represented by trades. For example, when you encounter a triangle pattern, a stop-loss could be placed $0.05 below the pattern.

### One strategy is to set two stop-losses:

1. Place a stop-loss order at a specific price level that suits your risk tolerance (the most money you can stand to lose).

2. If the trade makes an unexpected turn, immediately exit your position.

**Recommendation:** Paper trade using the strategy you came up with (for 50 to 100 trades), noting whether it was profitable and if it meets your expectations. If the strategy is working, proceed to trade it in a demo account in real time. Should your efforts be profitable over the course of at least two months in the simulated environment, begin day trading the strategy with real capital. If the strategy isn't profitable, start over.

Also, keep in mind that if trading on margin—which means

you're borrowing your investment funds from a brokerage firm—you're far more vulnerable to vicious price movements. Margin helps to swell the trading results not just of profits, but of losses as well. USE STOP-LOSSES.

## Fundamental strategies to consider:

- **Following the trend:** You buy when prices are rising or short-sell when they drop. The assumption is prices that have been rising or falling for some time will continue to do so.

- **Contrarian investing:** This strategy is based on doing the opposite of what most people are doing, and assumes that rising prices will reverse or that dropping prices will rise. You buy during the fall or short-sell during the rise.

- **Scalping:** You take advantage of small price gaps created by the bid-ask spread. You enter and exit your position fast—often within minutes or even seconds.

- **Trading on news:** Buy when good news breaks or short-sell when significant bad news is announced. The assumption, in either case, is that there will be greater volatility, which can lead to higher profits (or losses).

> **Final note:** Day trading isn't for the faint of heart. It requires a significant investment of time, is difficult to do skillfully and demands great discipline. This chapter was designed to help you create a profitable strategy. With much practice and **consistent performance evaluation**, you can significantly increase your chances of beating the odds.

## Notes

## Notes

_____

_____

_____

_____

_____

_____

_____

_____

_____

_____

_____

_____

_____

_____

_____

_____

_____

_____

_____

_____

# Chapter 8

# Looking for Agents

The first thing you have to do before looking for an agent is to decide what commodity or stock you would like to invest in. If it's real estate that you would like to invest in then ask fellow real estate investors if they have any real estate agents that they would recommend. Go to a real estate office, pick up papers that advertise properties for sale and talk to the agent on duty. Another good tip is to look for real estate investment courses. You could also approach mortgage brokers to see what your credit requirements may be and also if they know of any properties for sale. While you're talking to these people, ask for referrals to a real estate lawyer, as you'll need one to close purchase or sales. Ask all the people you talk to for referrals because having a big network of people in the real estate business will be a big advantage. Be prepared to turn any property down—even if the agent pushes you to buy.

If it's stocks and bonds you would like to buy, you may get some advice at your local bank. Research on the internet, or go to your library, as they have many books on this subject. Websites like Investopedia and Yahoo Finance provide good advice. If you're working at one of the larger companies, they may have financial personnel that could lead you in the right direction. As with all investments you must have some capital to start with and you may lose some of it if you make the wrong decisions. If you've done your homework, you may open an online account. You should ask the broker what their experience is and how long they've been in the business. You'll want to know if it's mutual funds, ETF or bonds and what the different fees are. Some questions are: How long do you have to invest? Are you a conservative person or are you more willing to take a risk? Do you have to leave the money in for a longer period or will there be larger fees if you want to redeem your money? What is your risk tolerance?

If it's commodities you want to invest in, do you know the language and have you done some study? There are four main ways to invest in commodities: 1. Invest directly in the commodity, 2. Use futures to invest, 3. Buy shares of ETF (exchange traded funds) and 4. Buy shares in stocks of companies that produce commodities. You also need to know how much money you can invest either as a lump sum or monthly through a PAC (pre-authorized contribution). Another idea is to check the internet for apps that guide you in commodities trading.

Investing in a commodity directly is fairly easy; just find a dealer who handles the particular commodity you want. Gold and silver are two commodities you can purchase directly, with the assistance of a dealer. Storing the commodity is fairly easy, as they come in bars or wafers and can be put directly into bank vault for safe-keeping until you want to dispose of them. Then you take them back to the dealer and they'll exchange them for cash. Other commodities are a little more difficult because of the storage and handling problems. Farmers deal with the grains directly because they have large storage bins out on their farms and they often wait for the prices to increase.

Futures are a way of investing in commodities, but you do need to find a stockbroker who deals in futures. This is a method of buying or selling at particular prices or dates in the future. You need to study the past rise and fall of a commodity that you're interested in. For some commodities you may have to buy large amounts, and this may stop a small investor from getting into some commodities. Futures can be good for the buyer and seller. A farmer may get a guaranteed price for a crop that he hasn't grown yet, and the food processer can buy that crop so he knows what his cost will be in the future.

ETFs (exchange traded funds) are another way to buy commodities. Some ETF companies buy physical commodities and offer shares to smaller investors. Some ETFs also use future contracts to sell to smaller investors.

Another strategy is buying shares of commodity producers. The oil and gas industry is one such area where many stocks are bought and sold, as the total net worth of the companies producing the commodity may be in the millions and it is out of reach for one person or entity to own the whole company. The price of the commodity may not determine the stock prices of the company. The internet is a good place to find both the price of the commodity and the price per share for companies dealing in that commodity.

Whether you're interested in investing in real estate, cryptocurrency or the stock market, online platforms like Udemy (https://www.udemy.com/topic/investing/) offer investing courses that can help you achieve your financial goals.

---

**Note: The CSC® (Canadian Securities Course)** is a baseline regulatory requirement to perform securities, mutual fund and alternative funds transactions (e.g. exchange-traded funds) in many financial services positions.

---

## You'll develop:

- A greater understanding of Canadian financial services

- Accuracy in assessing company, industry and market performance

- In-depth knowledge of codes of ethics and industry standards

- Knowledge, skills and tools to better serve yourself and your clients

- More knowledge regarding such financial instruments as derivatives, equities, managed products, structured products, etc

- Proficiency necessary to deal in alternative mutual funds products

**In addition to increasing your investment knowledge and skills, the course can lead to positions like:**

- Alternative mutual funds sales rep
- Bank or trust company officer
- Investment advisor
- Investment rep
- Financial planner
- Mutual funds sales rep

## Notes

## Notes

## Chapter 9

# How to Invest

One of the first things you need to do when you're thinking of investing is to decide what sort of investment and what industry you would like to get into. Something that may help you decide is the industry you work in or the occupation you have. An example is a construction worker who may want to get into the real estate industry as a renovator or builder. In this example a person may want to start small and renovate their own home. To do this they will probably have to buy their first property and it may need some renovation. This will increase the value of the house and that is called sweat equity, so the house is worth more than when the renovations started. As the person's net worth increases, they may want to go into renovating bigger houses and for someone else. They could also decide to construct new houses.

I recommend starting with a small amount and build from there as you get more education and experience. Borrowing money from friends, relatives and banks is called leverage. It will give you more money to get started but you have to look at the downside. If things go wrong, they tend to go twice as fast if you've borrowed and can't meet your commitments. One of the initial investments I recommend is your first family home because if and when you decide to sell and you have appreciation, the increase in value is not taxable. If you have invested in rental property or decide to flip the investment, the increase in value may be taxable. The increase in stock values may be taxable when you sell but any losses reduce your tax liability. You have to watch the year-end that you use.

If you have a small business and you are the only owner, the business is a sole proprietorship. You should carry insurance and get a business license. You have to remember that you're personally responsible for any debt incurred or injury to people or property. Good bookkeeping is necessary. If you should die, then your heir would be responsible for your debt and in a family situation this may not be something that you want to do. The problems could be mitigated by the purchase of life insurance.

You should have an accountant on your team as you may want to incorporate or go into partnership. Both of these methods of doing business make year-end an important thing to consider. In partnerships there are more things to consider as the other partners may not want to sell at the same time as you, so written partnership agreements are important. These agreements should contain information as to what happens in the event that a partner cannot fulfill their obligation, especially if disability or death occurs. If death occurs and things are not in writing, then you may wind up with a spouse or other beneficiary as a partner and they may not contribute to the partnership and create all sorts of problems for you.

If your business is incorporated, the management roles are usually better spelled out. If there were a death of one of the shareholders the shares might have to be sold but the person now holding the shares might not have much say in the day-to-day management of the company. When starting a business, the shares might be held in a private company. If you want to raise a lot of capital, you could go public with the shares. By this time, you would have lots of experience and help to do this.

These three types of business may have employees. They may have contracts with other companies to do work for them. These businesses will have sales with individuals and other companies. They will have liabilities that have to be looked after. If you are interested in business, I recommend that you get some business schooling and help before you start. If you know or can find a mentor, it would be very beneficial.

## Mutual Funds

### Step 1 - Decide Whether to Invest Actively or Passively

Actively managed funds are designed to beat the market. They're managed by professionals, and you pay a fee for the privilege. The problem is that it's tough to outperform the market in the long term. When you take these two facts into account, it's no wonder more investors are choosing passive funds as their vehicle of choice.

Passively managed funds charge fewer fees and those fees tend to be less expensive than those associated with active funds. They also mirror the market, so, for example, when the Standard & Poor's 500 index shows a gain of two points for the day, your S&P 500 fund would reflect this gain.

### Step 2 - Establish a Budget

When determining the amount of money you're going to invest, you need to feel comfortable leaving it untouched for at least five years (so as to ride out any market downturns). Patience and emotionless investing are the key words to remember here.

You should also be aware that mutual fund providers often require a minimum amount to open an account and begin investing. This can range from no initial amount to thousands of dollars.

Mutual funds are a low-cost way to build a diverse portfolio across stocks (the purpose is growth) and bonds (allows for lower but steadier returns). The question you must answer is what mix of funds is right for you? Generally, the closer you are to retirement age, the more holdings in conservative investments you will want to have—younger investors have more time to ride out riskier bets and inevitable reversals.

## Step 3 - Purchase Mutual Funds

You need a brokerage account. If you're enrolled in an employer-sponsored retirement account, it's likely that you're already investing in mutual funds. If not, you can buy directly from the company that created the fund(s) you're interested in. However, both of these options may limit your choice of funds.

In my experience, it's better to buy from an online brokerage, as many offer a wide selection of mutual funds from a significant range of fund companies. Should this be your choice, you'll want to consider:

- **Affordability.** You should expect to encounter two kinds of fees: broker transaction fees and fund charges (expense ratios, front-end loads and back-end loads).

- **Ease of use.** It's essential to understand and feel comfortable with the broker, the app and the website.

- **Fund choices.** Brokers can offer hundreds, if not thousands, of no-transaction-fee funds. These will include exchange-traded funds, or ETFs, which provide the same diversification as mutual funds but can be traded like stocks and target-date funds.

- **Research.** With all the choices mentioned above comes the need for more thinking, studying and research. It's vital to pick a broker who is willing to help you learn about a fund before investing your money.

## Step 4 - Investigate Your Costs

A company will charge you an annual fee (for fund management and other costs of running the fund), known as the expense ratio. For example, a fund with a 1.5% expense ratio will cost you $15 for every $1,000 you invest. These fees aren't always easy to identify but are worth the effort to understand because they can eat into your returns over time.

There can also be transaction charges associated with a fund, and some funds carry a sales fee that's paid to the broker selling the fund (called a sales load). Note: you can avoid these fees by investing with a broker who offers a list of no-transaction-fee mutual funds. Obviously all these fees affect your returns.

## Step 5 - Manage Your Portfolio

Once you've determined the mutual funds you want to buy, you'll need to think about how to manage your investment.

I suggest rebalancing your portfolio once a year—to keep it in line with your diversification plan. For example, if one of your investments had significant gains, you might consider selling off a portion of those gains and investing in something different to regain balance.

Don't chase performance, just stick to your investment plan. Remember, past performance isn't a guarantee of future performance.

### Examine the cost:

There are two broad types of mutual fund fees …

- **Annual operating expenses:** Ongoing fees that help pay for fund managers, accountants, legal fees, marketing, etc.

- **Shareholder fees:** commissions and other one-off costs that occur when you buy or sell shares.

You can find such details in your fund's prospectus, as filed with the SEC. Go to the fund's website and search for "annual fund operating expenses" and "shareholder fees."

## Annual Operating Expenses

These unavoidable fees, also known as mutual fund expense ratios or advisory fees, are generally 0.25% to 1.5% of your investment per year. The costs are higher for actively managed funds than for passively managed funds, and they may include:

- **Management fees:** what you pay the mutual fund managers and investment advisors.

- **12b-1 fees:** These fees pay for the marketing and selling of the fund, as well as other shareholder services and are capped at 1% of your investment.

- **Other expenses:** Accounting, administrative, custodial, legal and transfer agent expenses.

> **Note:** total annual fund operating expenses are expressed as a percentage of the fund's net average assets.

## Shareholder Fees

These expenses can include:

- **Account fee:** is often charged if your account balance slips below a specific (minimum) investment amount.

- **Exchange fee:** some funds charge if you transfer shares to different fund within the same investment company.

- **Purchase fee:** is paid to the fund at the time of purchase. This is distinct from a front-end sales load, which is paid to the broker for selling the fund.

- **Redemption fee:** charged when you sell shares within a short time after purchasing them (somewhere between a few days to a year, depending on the fund).

- **Sales loads:** Commissions you pay when you buy or sell mutual fund shares.

## Load Funds Versus No-Load Funds

A commission (percentage of your investment) that's paid when you purchase a fund is called a front-end load. A fee that's paid when you sell your investment is referred to as a back-end load.

Some funds charge no sales commissions (no-load funds).

Brokers may also charge additional transaction fees for buying or selling mutual funds (a flat fee that can range from $10 to $75).

> **Note:** As more investors look for low-cost ways to grow their investment portfolios, more brokers are offering no-load and no-transaction-fee mutual funds. However, even if the fund doesn't set sales loads, it still may charge redemption, exchange, account and purchase fees.

## Load Funds and Share Classes

Sales loads depend on what class of shares you buy:

- **A-class shares** have front-end sales loads, typically between 2% and 5% of total investment.

- **B-class shares** have back-end sales loads, which you don't pay until you sell your shares. The fees are charged for a specified period, usually up to seven years after the original purchase and decrease on a sliding scale depending on how soon you redeem your shares. It pays to stay invested. Also, B-class share funds typically charge higher ongoing annual fees than A-class share funds.

- **C-class shares** can carry commissions that are charged every year you own the fund, or they may have back-end sales loads.

## Individual Stocks and Bonds

Buying stocks or bonds involves finding a broker, earmarking funds for investing and deciding what you want to buy. Your first decision will be to find a trading platform or an automated investing service. Next, you need to determine how much money you can risk and still sleep at night. Interestingly, the most significant challenge will be deciding what stocks and bonds you should be buying.

## Where to Start Investing in Stocks

Picking stocks is like drawing blood. There's no easy way to do it. As mentioned previously, you would do well to select a cross-section of businesses that as a whole are bound to do well.

## How to Buy Stocks Online

Signing up to buy stocks online usually requires a home and work address, a phone number and a S.I.N. number. Fees will vary, but some platforms require no account minimums and charge zero trading fees.

> **Note:** Stocks are by nature volatile—they will rise and fall precipitously. Every prospectus you'll ever pick up includes the disclaimer, "past performance is no guarantee of future results." Why? Because it's true! Stocks tend to perform better than conservative investments like government bonds because investors are rewarded for risking more losses.

## Buying Stocks Without a Broker

These days it's possible to purchase stocks directly from large businesses like Pepsi through direct stock purchase plans (DSPPs). And given the fact that you can open a brokerage account in minutes and may be able to secure commission-free trading, there's no reason to avoid brokers.

But what about your risk tolerance?

Let's say that two people are considering investing $5,000. One will need the money in a couple of years for his child's university tuition. The other has ten times that amount in an opportunity and emergency fund. These two people have enormously different risk tolerances. The person with the looming tuition bill has no business in the stock market and should be in a conservative, safe place, like a high-interest cash account.

## Reducing Risk

The key to lowering investment risk is diversification. This equates to owning a broad portfolio of stocks across a diverse selection of economic sectors. That way, if one stock or sector suffers a significant setback, it will represent a tiny percentage of your capital.

## ETFs

Let's say you have an account with an online broker where you can buy and sell securities. I say this because buying individual ETFs won't be an option with an automated investing service.

If you're a first-time buyer, I suggest a low-cost index fund as an easy way to get a decent slice of the market. Such ETFs track an index, like the Standard & Poor's 500, and provide diversification without the necessity of buying many individual stocks.

For those of you who want other options, use the screening tools offered by brokerages to sift through the many available offerings. You can sort by asset type, geography, industry, trading performance or fund provider.

There are more than 2,000 ETFs listed in the U.S., so there will most likely be comparable funds even if you have a specific fund in mind. Your broker's website should have tools you can use to see how similar funds stack up on the following characteristics:

- **Administrative expenses.** These expenses cut into profit, so the lower the expense ratio, the better (for example, the average shareholder paid 0.23% in 2016).

- **Commission fees.** Most large brokerages offer commission-free trades for ETFs, or they'll have a selection of commission-free ETFs you can choose from.

- **Holdings.** You'll be able to see each of the companies in the fund. This allows for fund-to-fund comparison.

- **Performance.** While past performance doesn't indicate future returns, it can still be useful to see how ETF performance compares over time.

- **Trading prices.** Current prices dictate how many shares you can afford to buy.

- **Volume.** The number of shares that trade hands over a given period is an indicator of how popular a particular ETF is.

To invest in an ETF, you use its ticker symbol. Then, once you arrive at the trading section of your brokerage's website, buying ETFs is similar to the process of buying stocks. There are, however, some basics you need to know:

## Ticker Symbol

Be certain you have the right unique identifier for the ETF you want to buy.

## Price

The trading price is determined by 1. buyers who offer a bid, or the highest price they're willing to pay and 2. sellers who have an ask, or the lowest price they'll accept.

## Number of Shares

This is the number of shares you wish to buy or sell.

## Order Type

- **Limit order:** This is a request to buy only at a specific price (or lower).

- **Market order:** You are indicating that you wish to buy immediately at the best available price.

- **Stop-limit order:** When the stop price is reached, the trade turns into a limit order.

- **Stop order:** You want to buy the complete order once a specified price has been reached (the stop price).

## Commission

This is the price per trade the brokerage will charge you for its service. However, most large brokerages now offer commission-free ETF trades.

## Funding Source

This is the bank account that you linked to your brokerage account. It's crucial to have sufficient funds to cover the total cost of your trades.

> **Note:** Double-check that everything's correct. Ensure the ticker symbol and order type are accurate and that you haven't made a terrible error (eg. typing 1,000 shares when you intended to buy 100).

ETFs can help form a well-diversified portfolio and serve as the first step in a long-lasting investment in the markets. There's no need to continually check how your ETFs are performing, but you can easily do so when you need to by checking the ticker symbol on your brokerage's website or Google.

Talk to Thomas about your financial needs at **tombhur@gmail. com**.

## Notes

_____

_____

_____

_____

_____

_____

_____

_____

_____

_____

_____

_____

_____

_____

_____

_____

_____

_____

_____

_____

## *Notes*

_____

_____

_____

_____

_____

_____

_____

_____

_____

_____

_____

_____

_____

_____

_____

_____

_____

_____

_____

_____

# Chapter 10

# Making it Count

Salting away money should be a decision you make early in life because the sooner you start the more time you have to put something together and also recover from any mistakes or problems that may arise. But even if you're older, it's never too late to get started. The time when you could work for one employer and wind up at retirement with a good pension is over. Even working for the government doesn't guarantee a good retirement because governments are changing and downsizing. The whole work environment leaves you responsible for your retirement.

And I cannot stress enough that getting a basic education (grade twelve) is the place to begin. This should be accomplished by age twenty. From here you either have to go to work or enroll in further education. Entering the work force is good if you don't have the marks for college or university. Entering college or university means many years of education, which can create huge liabilities due to student loans. Professionals like doctors and lawyers can be in university for ten or more years. Another option is getting into trades, which usually requires three to five years of study to attain journeyman status. Even jobs like truck driving require a fair amount of education because you don't just climb in a truck and drive, you have to obtain a license. Besides the license, you have to know how to load the truck and remember lots of rules and regulations. Truck driving is an in-demand occupation, and it can cost up to ten thousand dollars just to obtain your license

If you're still in high school, there may be the option of taking a pre-apprenticeship or first year while still in high school. This sets you up for a good occupation, and there are many opportunities available in the next few years. You may get involved in management or work with or for other very successful people. Most people today are going to have six or more occupations in their working lives. Once you become a tradesman you have the possibility of many other occupations. You may want to become an estimator, expeditor, draftsmen, owner or take up another occupation.

Similar things could happen to truck drivers as they have some of the same chances to change occupations in the transportation field. Also they may want to start their own business and become owner/operators, which gives them the ability to earn more money.

All of life requires further education to open up opportunities that aren't available when you're just leaving school. As well as having good occupations, this schooling may open up investment opportunities in financial instruments as well as business. Good planning will bring about a good return but you have to also expect unexpected problems. A network of professional and business people will help resolve many of the problems life may throw at you.

## Create Net Worth Quarterly or Semi-Annually

Going back to the topic of money: any savings or investment program needs to produce positive cash flow or build equity. How do you know this is happening? I refer you to the budget forms from earlier. They can give you a snapshot of your financial situation at any given moment; they can help you determine your net worth. Now, you don't want to be doing that amount of work on a daily or even a weekly basis. I do, however, strongly suggest that you crunch your numbers at least every three to six months. That way you know in which direction your finances are heading and what, if anything, you need to do differently. Blowing your budget with too many restaurant lunches? Make an adjustment. Investments not doing as well as expected? Do you have time to ride things out, or do you need to reposition yourself in the market—perhaps getting into something a little safer? Do you have a separate emergency fund that's in a money market or savings account? And are you managing to stick to the budget you last did?

## Get a Mentor

As I mentioned, a network of professional or business people can give you the knowledge you need to deal with many of life's challenges. One of the best relationships you can build is with a mentor, someone who already has the skills and achievements you yearn for. Now, it's important to realize that a mentor doesn't have to be with you in person. In this heady age of computers, the world is at your fingertips. I've also learned incredible lessons reading books and listening to audio tapes. I think about the work of Earl Nightingale, in particular. Raymond Aaron has also been instrumental in my success.

## Get Started

The whole point, though, is to get started. Anything you do regarding the acquisition of skills, knowledge and money in the short term will reward you in the long term. It doesn't matter how little you can put away or how old you are. There's no substitute for education, experience and what they used to call a rainy-day fund.

Learning in any form has, at least in my life, always been worth the time and money spent to acquire it. And without a cash reserve you can't take advantage of opportunities or deal with emergencies. Oh, you can rely on credit cards or bank loans, but they create a whole other set of problems, don't they? Over the years I've had to use and then rebuild my rainy day fund many times. But it has limited my debt enough that I've not had to worry about high interest rates and ongoing payments for money spent that I didn't have.

So invest in yourself! Do something today to increase your knowledge, expand your skills and set aside some money. You'll be glad you did.

Unsure? Make your first decision: contact Thomas for help at **tombhur@gmail.com**.

## Notes

## Notes

_____

_____

_____

_____

_____

_____

_____

_____

_____

_____

_____

_____

_____

_____

_____

_____

_____

_____

_____

_____

_____

# Summary

This book is being completed in the middle of the Coronavirus pandemic. This pandemic enforces the belief that people need to do better planning of their finances. The first thing people need is to learn some of the acronyms used in the handling of money. A good mentor can be very helpful in the handling of your money. When you're starting out, it's necessary to live within your means so that you can put six to twelve months of money for expenses into an emergency account. This emergency account could be in a bank but a good supply of cash should be in a safe where it is readily available. You should be putting at least ten percent of your income into savings, and when you have a good supplement to back you up, then you can look at investing. There are some investment ideas in this book but remember it's cash that is the most important. If you have a job, it's always good to look for ways to make more money on a side hustle enterprise. As you go through life, look for ways to get more financial knowledge as laws and economic conditions are always changing. Look for ways to save from paying income tax by utilizing registered retirement plans.

Some mentors can be found on the internet and they offer different free advice in the form of webinars and pdf reports as well as free personal presentations. Some Canadians are Raymond Aaron, Bob Proctor and Dan Loc. I have been a fan of Raymond

Aaron for over thirty years. These people and many others can be found on the internet.

I would like to acknowledge Raymond Aaron and Clayton Bye as well as Raymond Aaron's staff in the production of this book.

—Thomas B. Hurley

Please contact Thomas Hurley at<br>Tombhur@gmail.com

www.ingramcontent.com/pod-product-compliance
Lightning Source LLC
Chambersburg PA
CBHW062014200326
41519CB00017B/4797